GNU Linux Ubuntu 10.04 LTS Server Edition

Ubuntu Server for Small Business
Pocket Guide

Learn how to use Ubuntu to create and administer a powerful, modern and complete system suitable to school and to small and very small business.

Stefano Giro

The author

Stefano Giro is a freelancer computer professional who deals in business of system engineer, programmer and consultant at small and medium-sized business in north-eastern Italy.

His blog, from which the material of this book in part is derived, is available at:

http://www.stenoit.com

ISBN 978-1-4475-1719-1

First edition : March 2011

Table of contents

Chapter 1
Getting started   19

Chapter 2
The sudo command   23

Chapter 3
SSH Server   27

Chapter 4
LDAP Server   31

Chapter 5
DNS & DHCP Server   45

Chapter 6
Firewall Server   63

Chapter 7
LAMP Server   71

Chapter 8
File Server 77

Chapter 9
Mail Server   119

Chapter 10
Proxy Server   151

Chapter 11
Time Server 171

Chapter 12
Snapshot Backup 173

Chapter 13
Instant Messaging Server   189

Chapter 14
Fax Server   217

Chapter 15
VPN Server   227

Chapter 16
Conclusions 241

Preface

The situation of a school or a small or very small business where the desire to save money without sacrificing security or efficiency is a primary need, is the perfect environment for solutions based on GNU Linux, an operating system very widespread and with proven efficiency, security and scalability.

This doesn't mean that Linux is not suitable for larger companies, but in this case scenarios are more complex and a solution of this type may not be the best one. For example, if our users grow up to become a hundred or more, you should at least split the workload across multiple servers and spend more time on initial tuning to ensure efficiency.

But we don't worry here. Our target are installations that may have from two to about twenty users, where the needs are moderate and where the fact that there are no software licensing costs will be appreciated.

Which Linux distribution use?

The answers to this question can be many, and all with a piece of truth.

However, what we should keep in mind is that the used software is always the same and "distro-agnostic", an abstruse term in order to indicate that they generally do not prefer some distribution in particular.

But even so, my personal recommendation is to settle one of the most commonly used: Ubuntu, Debian, CentOS, RedHat, SLES or OpenSUSE because they give us more effective guarantee of updates and a considerable amount of documentation online.

Here we will use the distrowatch leader: **Ubuntu 10.04 Server Long Term Support (LTS) version**, published in April 2010 and that it assures us updates until 2015. Reader beware: here we will not use any facilities to configure and install the various services, our tool will be almost exclusively the *system shell bash*.

I think this approach *is necessary* to learn to manage professionally a Linux Server. After we have learned to use this maybe primitive system, we may also decide to use a beautiful GUI with animated icons if we like. But if this is not possible, we should be able to give ourselves the same, and to do so the only thing we need is a connection shell with a nice blinking prompt, efficient even if we are on the opposite side of the world.

Finally, I hope will forgive me some imperfection in the translation: this book is self-publish and the English is not my primary language.

Good reading and good installation at all!

Stefano Giro.

Inside

Here is what we are going to achieve following this guide chapter by chapter. Reader beware: the services installed are often linked together, then you may be unable to achieve a single service without any of the others. For example we cannot install a Webmail unless we install a LAMP server, and Chapter 4 (*LDAP Server), is necessary,* because all services that require authentication will use a common database users stored on his tree, both in the case we choose the *open source* solution *(OpenLDAP),* and the *commercial (Active Directory),*

I tried, when possible, not to go too much into details but at the same time, trying not to be too trivial. Sometimes I have come down a bit more in depth sometimes less. What I recommend, and I don't tire to repeat, is that if something isn't clear, should be considered a good thing to acquire additional documentation, especially when there are services that should ensure a minimum level of security.

Chapter 1 – Getting Started
Before you begin it is necessary to prepare the machine and understand the conventions used in this guide. In this book is not described the basic installation of Ubuntu Server. Reading this chapter we will understand what are the minimum requirements needed to use this guide.

Chapter 2 – The SUDO command
Overview on the functioning and the purpose of the *sudo* command, why it was adopted and strengths and weaknesses compared to the traditional model with *root* and *su.*

Chapter 3 – SSH Server
Secure Shell service is required for installation and management of servers and workstations remotely.

Chapter 4 – LDAP Server
The LDAP server is the hub of all services offered in this guide. It shall be the depositary of user accounts, and all services will support it for authentication. Necessary to obtain a *Single Signon*, and to have a single database for users and passwords.
In this chapter we will see both how to create a standalone LDAP server using *OpenLDAP*, and how to use an important external and commercial service like *Microsoft Active Directory.*

Chapter 5 – DNS & DHCP Server
A simple *Caching DNS and DHCP* service to provide IP resolution to the PC of our network. This service is indispensable. Two solution will be shown, the simplest one is *dnsmasq* and the most diffused coupled is *Bind & DHCPD*.

Chapter 6 – Firewall Server
Security is important. Here we will learn to configure our server so that it controls traffic between our private network and Internet.
It is indispensable for many other services and absolutely impossible to ignore.

Chapter 7 – LAMP Server
In order to provide special services (e.g. Web Mail) we must have a web server with PHP and database support (LAMP). In this chapter we will learn how to install a simple but functional one for our purposes.

Chapter 8 – File Server
This is one of the most important parts and one of the main reasons why a server is installed in the company. Here we will configure a full authentication to OpenLDAP and Active Directory. We see also how to solve some issues and specific cases that may arise when implementing such solutions.

Chapter 9 – Mail Server
Here we will learn how to make SMTP, POP3, IMAP and Webmail service to fit our network with a modern e-mail service with antispam and antivirus filters.

Chapters 10 – Proxy Server
Learn how to control web browsing is important. In this chapter we will create a proxy caching service in order to speed up browsing, complete with integrated user authentication with Samba/LDAP and Active Directory, control over the visited websites and automatically configuration of the browser with WPAD feature.

Chapter 11 – Time Server
A simple service to synchronize date and time on the whole network, taken from Internet.

Chapter 12 – Snapshot Backup
Saving our data is important. Here we will see and understand how to achieve a modern, fast and efficient backup solution using only software tools already included in the operating system with cheap and common USB hard disks.

Chapter 13 – Instant Messaging Server

Chat services are very popular on the Internet and are becoming important even within a company. In this chapter we will see two alternative solutions about how to implement a private chat server integrated with OpenLDAP or Active Directory.

Chapter 14 – Fax Server

Many people think that the fax is an antiquated tool of communication but in practice this is not true. On Small Business this service is still used very much and we cannot ignore it.

Chapter 15 – VPN Server

In this chapter we will learn how to configure a basic VPN service to allow external users to access securely through a secure connection to our services from a remote location via Internet.

Chapter 16 – Conclusions

Credits and links to official sites of the software used.

1

Getting started

This pocket guide contains information about how to install and configure several services on Ubuntu 10.04 LTS in order to achieve a small, modern and efficient Server. Is a simple step by step guide to configure and customize our system. The various sections should not be necessarily executed in order but according to the need.

Requirements:

- ✔ The base installation of Ubuntu Server 10.04 was created without selecting any additional service when we are asked. If we have doubts we can follow the official guide that we find on the site of Canonical LTD.
- ✔ We have two network adapters: one connected to our internal network and one to the xDSL router.
- ✔ A working Internet connection.
- ✔ A basic knowledge of Ubuntu or Linux in general and of the covered topics.

This is not a complete guide to services used, to deepen the knowledge I would refer you to the official guides of the packages themselves. The main purpose is to give a track to follow, the possible combinations are so many that it is virtually impossible to treat every single need.

I repeat that, when possible, any GUI to configure the system won't be used, we will use *only a bash shell*, in this way we would have the great advantage of being able to manage and resolve most problems of our server even remotely.

Finally, although it seems like an obvious thing, I want to point out that: we should try to understand at least the basic things we're doing without just a copy & paste commands. For example, if we follow the Guide on services DNS or LDAP, first of all we should inform us at least on what they are. It is dangerous to install a server without knowing the topics covered; therefore at the first difficulty we will curse the moment we decided to use Linux.

Preparing the System

Conventions

- ✔ eth0 is the Ethernet adapter that is connected to the Internet (or WAN). It has a static IP address (required for the Mail Server) or provider-assigned using DHCP. Here we assume that is, 212.239.29.208 with gateway 212.239.29.10 and netmask 255.255.255.0.
- ✔ 192.168.20.0/24 is the internal network
- ✔ eth1 is the Ethernet adapter that is connected to our internal LAN and 192.168.20.1 static IP address.
- ✔ our server is called *sbs*
- ✔ our domain is *stenoit.com*
- ✔ our administrative user is *sbsadmin*

Update packages

Before starting we update weekend our packages to the latest version. From the shell we run commands:

```
sudo apt-get update
sudo apt-get upgrade
```

Additional packages

There are useful packages that are better to install. For me were these:

```
sudo apt-get install sysv-rc-conf mc joe build-essential pkg-config
```

Domain and resolution

Edit the file */etc/resolv.conf* where we define the domain and DNS.

```
sudo nano /etc/resolv.conf
```

And let's get this, the specified DNS are those very fast and used to OpenDNS. We can, alternatively, use any of our provider.

```
search stenoit.com
domain stenoit.com
```

```
nameserver 208.67.222.222
nameserver 208.67.220.220
```

Hosts file

We must fix the */etc/hosts* file so that it locally resolves the name of the server:

```
sudo nano /etc/hosts
```

Making it become so:

```
127.0.0.1        localhost
192.168.20.1     sbs sbs.stenoit.com stenoit.com
```

Configuring network adapters

We configure our network adapters as by *Conventions*. To do this we edit the file:

```
sudo nano /etc/network/interfaces
```

We should see something like this:

```
# This file describes the network interfaces available on your system
# and how to activate them. For more information, see interfaces(5).

# The loopback network interface
auto lo
iface lo inet loopback

# The external network interface
auto eth0
iface eth0 inet dhcp
```

at this time to eth0 the IP address is assigned dynamically, while we want that both network interfaces on the server have one fixed.
Let's comment the lines relating to eth0 and add the following:

```
# The primary network interface
#auto eth0
#iface eth0 inet dhcp

# External Interfaccia
auto eth0
iface eth0 inet static
        address 212.239.29.208
        netmask 255.255.255.0
        network 212.239.29.0
        broadcast 212.239.29.255
        gateway 212.239.29.10

# Internal Interface
auto eth1
iface eth1 inet static
```

```
address 192.168.20.1
netmask 255.255.255.0
network 192.168.20.0
broadcast 192.168.20.255
```

Without reboot now disable interfaces:

```
sudo ifdown eth0
sudo ifdown eth1
```

enable them immediately after:

```
sudo ifup eth0
sudo ifup eth1
```

Or, more simply, we can achieve the same result by restarting network services:

```
sudo /etc/init.d/networking restart
```

Now with the command:

```
ifconfig
```

we should get something like this:

```
eth0    Link encap:Ethernet  HWaddr 00:0c:29:43:47:dd
        inet addr:212.239.29.208 Bcast:212.239.29.255  Mask:255.255.255.0
        inet6 addr: fe80::20c:29ff:fe43:47dd/64 Scope:Link
        UP BROADCAST RUNNING MULTICAST  MTU:1500  Metric:1
        RX packets:33651 errors:0 dropped:0 overruns:0 frame:0
        TX packets:20315 errors:0 dropped:0 overruns:0 carrier:0
        collisions:0 txqueuelen:1000
        RX bytes:45577333 (43.4 MB)  TX bytes:1597438 (1.5 MB)
        Interrupt:17 Base address:0x2000

eth1    Link encap:Ethernet  HWaddr 00:0c:29:43:47:e7
        inet addr:192.168.20.1  Bcast:192.168.20.255  Mask:255.255.255.0
        inet6 addr: fe80::20c:29ff:fe43:47e7/64 Scope:Link
        UP BROADCAST RUNNING MULTICAST  MTU:1500  Metric:1
        RX packets:0 errors:0 dropped:0 overruns:0 frame:0
        TX packets:6 errors:0 dropped:0 overruns:0 carrier:0
        collisions:0 txqueuelen:1000
        RX bytes:0 (0.0 B)  TX bytes:468 (468.0 B)
        Interrupt:18 Base address:0x2080

lo      Link encap:Local Loopback
        inet addr:127.0.0.1  Mask:255.0.0.0
        inet6 addr: ::1/128 Scope:Host
        UP LOOPBACK RUNNING  MTU:16436  Metric:1
        RX packets:0 errors:0 dropped:0 overruns:0 frame:0
        TX packets:0 errors:0 dropped:0 overruns:0 carrier:0
        collisions:0 txqueuelen:0
        RX bytes:0 (0.0 B)  TX bytes:0 (0.0 B)
```

Our network configuration is complete.

2

The sudo command

How many times we had to do with this command? Who uses Ubuntu regularly, would like to dedicate a special key on the keyboard...

Anyone who has used Linux, or Unix, generally knows that there is a super user *root* (UID=0), used to administer the system that *have total access to each and every feature.*

However it is good practice to use a less privileged user to do the daily work. Where, then, there was no need to perform administrative tasks, you should open a terminal by starting only at that time a session as the *root* user, or use the **su** command to become temporarily such.

Ubuntu uses a slightly different approach to carry out administrative tasks, based on using the **sudo** command, *leaving disabled the super user root.* With sudo the administrative tasks will be played by using the same habitual user's password with low privileges.

In each of the two approaches (**sudo** Vs **su**) there are pros and cons, let's analyze them briefly.

Su

Fans of *su* model, i.e. with root account enabled, argue that this is safer because the administrative level is obtained after inserting two passwords, user password and the root password.

This is because, as is common practice, a remote terminal does not accept a direct connection with superuser root, forcing the administrator to login first with a normal user and only later with *su* for jumping to administrative tasks.

If not, it turns out immediately the partial weakness of this approach. The name of the super user *is already known*, a hacker should only attempt to uncover their password.

If we prefer however this traditional administrative model, with Ubuntu we must remember *to turn off remote superuser access* (we will see how in Chapter 3) and to enable the user by assigning a password:

```
sudo passwd root
```

If we change opinion, we can disable it:

```
sudo passwd -l root
```

or then re-enable them again with:

```
sudo passwd -u root
```

Sudo

With *sudo (superuser do)*, unlike what happens with *su*, we are forced to a controlled execution of each individual command.

To perform administrative operations we must type *"sudo"* before each command, as we have seen just above if you enabled root:

```
sudo passwd root
```

the system, so, will ask us the password of the current user by storing it for a short period of time, sufficient to permit us to execute commands close together without bother us repeatedly prompts for credentials.

This approach reduces the time where users are in the system as administrator, reduces the risk of inadvertently malicious commands to launch the system, and increases the possibilities of research and analysis on the system log of commands.

Reading beware: If someone discovers the password of a user who has permission to use sudo, *he could obtain unconditional access to the system*. So a particular attention to the choice of password for this user must be paid!

With sudo, however, the name of the user who has administrative privileges is not a foregone conclusion: it is so more difficult to attack the system since the malicious hacker must first locate the user than later   attack his password.

Another advantage is the ability to delegate some administrative tasks to other users, because we do not have the need to give them the root password. The administrator can assign to any user, even temporarily, special privileges and then delete them when no longer needed.

For example, here's how to assigns to "user1" the privilege to turn off our servers. Typing:

```
sudo visudo
```

/etc/sudoers file is opened using the System Editor (typically *vim*). *visudo* controls how much we write on this very important file avoiding possible errors.

Now we insert at the bottom:

```
user1  localhost=/sbin/shutdown -h now
```

Save the file and exit. Now *"user1"* is able to perform the *shutdown* command, only however from the local machine *(localhost)*.

All transactions will be stored in the log file */var/log/auth.log*, allowing us to monitor what has been done using *sudo*.

Conclusions

Which solution take then? We saw the pros and cons of each of the two solution and I personally think that, whatever opinion of each one of us on that system, it is still preferable to rely on the default solution proposed by who has packaged the system, in this case Ubuntu.

From now on, we logon at the console with our user *sbsadmin* and use *sudo* to administrative tasks, having seen, however, that the decision can be easily changed. If some services require the presence of the root user, switch to the alternative solution is very simple and quick.

3

SSH Server

To administer the server remotely, or from a machine on the same network, we need to install and configure *OpenSSH* that allows us to perform our duties from anywhere with a secure shell without constricting to position ourselves in front of the physical console.

Furthermore, we will learn also how it is even possible, from the Internet, use it to access to internal machines to our company and establish a secure tunnel.

Installation

Installing and starting the service:

```
sudo apt-get install openssh-server openssh-client
```

Now **any host/IP address** can attempt to connect remotely.

Configuration

In order to reduce the security risks we open the configuration file:

```
sudo nano /etc/ssh/sshd_config
```

If we didn't need to remotely access we may restrict access only to hosts on the internal network:

```
ListenAddress 192.168.20.1
```

or allow only particulate users, for example, *sbsadmin* from anywhere, *user1* only from host 192.168.20.10:

```
AllowUsers sbsadmin user1@192.168.20.10
```

But what is really important if we chose to enable root (see Chapter 2) is to refuse its direct connection.

```
DenyUsers root
```

In this way to administer our server with SSH we'll have to connect with another user and then use the "su" command.

If instead we kept the default Ubuntu configuration, this setting is not necessary, since the super user is disabled.

Finally, to make operational changes to the configuration, we must restart the service:

```
sudo /etc/init.d/ssh restart
```

SSH Tunneling

OpenSSH is a powerful tool that not only provides a secure shell with which administer our servers.

I think it's another very interesting and useful feature: the ability to create a secure tunnel that, through our server, we can also *remotely access the company's internal workstations* to the domain stenoit.com otherwise unreachable from the public network.

Usually the first solution we think about when we speak of "Remote Assistance" to the clients of the network is using the RDP Services (included in Windows XP and later versions) or VNC (cross-platform software, free and easily downloadable from the Internet). They allow us to take control of the user's desktop and operate as if we were sitting in front of their computers.

Imagine so to be connected to the Internet from home with our PC and want to help a hypothetical user on workstation named *"wks01"* with IP 192.168.20.10 within the company, and on which I have previously allowed at least one of those services (RDP or VNC).

With our ssh client we can of course open a shell on *sbs.stenoit.com*, but we can do it in a particular way by *creating an encrypted tunnel between our PC and wks01*, using our server as a "bridge".

Let's see how.

Linux

Let's assume that our PC is equipped with Linux and we want to access with VNC (port 5900) to wks01. From the shell just type:

```
ssh -L5900:wks01:5900 sbsadmin@sbs.stenoit.com
```

or using the IP addresses:

```
ssh -L5900:192.168.20.10:5900 sbsadmin@212.239.29.208
```

the system, of course, requires password of user *sbsadmin*.

Apparently anything doesn't seem happen but instead now, until the ssh session is active, we can access to the desktop of a VNC client wks01 by connecting us to the local port 5900. SSH will route the communication safely to port 5900 of the workstation through the tunnel just created.

We can of course use any port/service like RDP (port 3389) for the remote desktop:

```
ssh -L13389:wks01:3389 sbsadmin@sbs.stenoit.com
```

the local port (in this case 13389) is arbitrary, we can put any valid value being careful, though, that any other service is running on the same.

In this situation by typing as address on our RDP client:

```
localhost:13389
```

We will see appear the wks01 remote desktop.

Windows

If the remote machine from which we access has some version of Windows installed, we can use the freeware **putty** ssh client, downloadable from this address:

```
http://www.chiark.greenend.org.uk/~sgtatham/putty/download.html
```

does not require installation, just the simple executable.

Putty can be used through the graphical GUI or directly from the command line with a syntax almost identical to the one seen before:

```
putty -L 5900:wks01:5900 sbsadmin@sbs.stenoit.com
```

The features don't change absolutely compared to Linux, they are the same.

Conclusions

So we have seen how remotely, providing only the credentials of a ssh access to our servers, using OpenSSH we can potentially access to any internal company service, a database, a web server, simple shares samba/windows, or whatever.

Besides the obvious advantages of this technique, I hope you *have also under-stood how much dangerous can be OpenSSH in the hands of wrong people*, since it provides a real "master key" of our private network. Therefore the good habit **to choose a non-trivial password**, to disable the root user or at least do not allow its direct access to the server as explained before, become really important.

4

LDAP Server

The LDAP Server (*Lightweight Directory Access Protocol)* is the hub of most of the solutions proposed in this book. The services we install in later chapters will use it, especially for authenticating users.

We analyze two alternative solutions: the first one will use the Linux server with the open source *OpenLDAP*, the second one will use an external service, in our case the widespread and commercial *Microsoft Active Directory.*

OpenLDAP

Why do we install this service? For its great versatility and convenience. LDAP is essentially a hierarchical database that can be used to store everything you want to manage through a shareable database, also via network between multiple systems.

By installing an LDAP server (in our case *OpenLDAP*) we have the ability to centralize data management, whether they are user accounts, groups, passwords, or whatever. There is so a unique coupled user/password to access any service, File Server, Mail Server, Instant Messaging and so on.

Creating a new user or even simply by changing your password, we can be sure that this is automatically synchronized for each service.

In other words, OpenLDAP will allow us to realize the so-called *Single Signon*, the Holy Grail of any network administrator.

OpenLDAP is a powerful and complex service, without any difficulty it can scale across multiple servers while maintaining replicas synchronized data.

I'd like to make it clear, once again, that the aim of this book is not to provide a detailed guide to the operation or to the terms of a directory service based on

LDAP. Here we only provide a step-by-step guide that will enable us to achieve the desired target. Additional information can be found on the official site.

Installation

We install the needed packages:

```
sudo apt-get install slapd ldap-utils db4.8-util
```

We are waiting until apt ends the installation of packages.

Configuration

The configuration is a little bit more complicated than the old Ubuntu LTS, because *debconf* now takes only a "reset" parameters. To set manually administrator, domain and password we must proceed in another way. In fact we see:

```
sudo dpkg-reconfigure slapd
```

in sequence only the following information is required:

```
Omit OpenLDAP server configuration? => <No>
Do you want the database to be removed when slapd is purged? => <No>
Allow LDAPv2 protocol? => <No>
```

The reason for this is that now OpenLDAP, rather than save the configuration in ordinary files as happened in the past, uses a separate directory (*"cn=config"*) for the configuration called *"Directory Information Tree (DIT)*. The *"DIT"* allows you to dynamically configure the daemon *"slapd"* allowing also quick changes to schemes, indexes and ACL without the need to stop and restart the service.

Although this is a definite advantage for he continuity of service, the configuration is a little more complicated because we must use ldap shell commands to configure the service.

But let's see how to do it, starting with the move in the correct directory:

```
cd /etc/ldap
```

Schemes

Let's start by manually adding the "schemes" required:

```
sudo ldapadd -Y EXTERNAL -H ldapi:/// -f /etc/ldap/schema/cosine.ldif
sudo ldapadd -Y EXTERNAL -H ldapi:/// -f /etc/ldap/schema/inetorgperson.ldif
sudo ldapadd -Y EXTERNAL -H ldapi:/// -f /etc/ldap/schema/nis.ldif
```

After each command we should get something like this (for instance for "cosine" scheme):

```
SASL/EXTERNAL authentication started
SASL username: gidNumber=0+uidNumber=0,cn=peercred,cn=external,cn=auth
SASL SSF: 0
adding new entry "cn=cosine,cn=schema,cn=config"
```

Database

Let's start now the creation of a series of LDIF files that allows us to configure OpenLDAP in easiest way. The first of the series is that concerning the BDB database used as back-end:

```
sudo nano db.ldif
```

Insert the following, paying particular attention to the bold words that define our domain, the LDAP administrator user and password:

```
# Load dynamic backend modules
dn: cn=module{0},cn=config
objectClass: olcModuleList
cn: module
olcModulepath: /usr/lib/ldap
olcModuleload: {0}back_hdb

# Create the database
dn: olcDatabase={1}hdb,cn=config
objectClass: olcDatabaseConfig
objectClass: olcHdbConfig
olcDatabase: {1}hdb
olcDbDirectory: /var/lib/ldap
olcSuffix: dc=stenoit,dc=com
olcRootDN: cn=admin,dc=stenoit,dc=com
olcRootPW: ldappwd
olcDbConfig: {0}set_cachesize 0 2097152 0
olcDbConfig: {1}set_lk_max_objects 1500
olcDbConfig: {2}set_lk_max_locks 1500
olcDbConfig: {3}set_lk_max_lockers 1500
olcLastMod: TRUE
olcDbCheckpoint: 512 30
olcDbIndex: uid eq,pres,sub
olcDbIndex: cn,sn,mail pres,eq,approx,sub
olcDbIndex: objectClass eq
```

When the file is available, we use *ldapadd:*

```
sudo ldapadd -Y EXTERNAL -H ldapi:/// -f db.ldif
```

Basic configuration and admin

In the previous paragraph we have defined the access password *("ldappwd")*. Now we need to generate the MD5 hash and store it in this format on the database. Let's use the command:

```
slappasswd -h {MD5} -s ldappwd
```

that gives us:

```
{MD5}1AdI/WviFyu0uh+L61C14g==
```

That is what we are going to insert in the following file that will provide a basic *slapd* configuration by defining also user and administrator password:

```
sudo nano base.ldif
```

We insert the following lines:

```
dn: dc=stenoit,dc=com
objectClass: dcObject
objectclass: organization
o: stenoit.com
dc: stenoit
description: StenoIT Corporation

dn: cn=admin,dc=stenoit,dc=com
objectClass: simpleSecurityObject
objectClass: organizationalRole
cn: admin
userPassword:{MD5}1AdI/WviFyu0uh+L6lC14g==
description: LDAP administrator
```

and then we load the configuration:

```
sudo ldapadd -Y EXTERNAL -H ldapi:/// -f base.ldif
```

ACL

Now we set the ACL to access the directory using, later, the default *"cn=admin, cn=config"*. We create the file:

```
sudo nano config.ldif
```

containing:

```
dn: cn=config
changetype: modify

dn: olcDatabase={0}config,cn=config
changetype: modify
add: olcRootDN
olcRootDN: cn=admin,cn=config

dn: olcDatabase={0}config,cn=config
changetype: modify
add: olcRootPW
olcRootPW: {MD5}1AdI/WviFyu0uh+L6lC14g==

dn: olcDatabase={0}config,cn=config
changetype: modify
delete: olcAccess
```

And we load them:

```
sudo ldapadd -Y EXTERNAL -H ldapi:/// -f config.ldif
```

Now we can define the read/write ACL. Let's do it again with another *LDIF* file:

```
sudo nano acl.ldif
```

containing (**warning: olcAccess commands must be on a single line!**):

```
dn: olcDatabase={1}hdb,cn=config
add: olcAccess
olcAccess: to attrs=userPassword,shadowLastChange by dn="cn=admin,dc=stenoit,dc=com"
         write by anonymous auth by self write by * none
olcAccess: to dn.base="" by * read
olcAccess: to * by dn="cn=admin,dc=stenoit,dc=com" write by * read
```

We just have to upload it:

```
sudo ldapmodify -x -D cn=admin,cn=config -W -f acl.ldif
```

Pay attention that I have now also defined the user with the parameter *"-D"* (on our example password is *"ldappwd"*).

If we have make something wrong we can repeat the whole procedure again being careful to remove and reinstall the package **slapd**:

```
apt-get remove slapd --purge
apt-get install slapd
```

nsswitch.conf

The *Network Services Switch* determines the order of the performed searches when you request some information, just as the file */etc/host.conf* determines how to perform searches of the hosts. For example, the line:

```
hosts: files dns ldap
```

specifies that host lookup functions should:

1. look in the local */etc/hosts* file
2. make a request to the DNS server
3. use the LDAP server.

At that point, if no match is found, an error is returned.

In our case we must instruct *nsswitch* because, as second option, it uses LDAP for the resolution of users, passwords and groups.

We can also do it manually by editing the file:

```
sudo nano /etc/nsswitch.conf
```

replacing "*compat*" with "*files ldap*":

```
passwd:          files ldap
shadow:          files ldap
group:           files ldap
```

The priority is always to local files of Linux (*/etc/passwd* for users, */etc/shadow* for passwords and */etc/group* for groups), in this way we can authenticate the *sbsadmin* user even if the LDAP server is unreachable or disabled.

PAM

PAM *(Pluggable Authentication Modules)* is a mechanism to integrate multiple authentication schemes at low level in a single high-level API, allowing programs that require a form of authentication, to be written regardless of he authentication scheme used below.

Instead of manually changing all its configuration files (*/etc/pam.d/**), in this case we will use a Python script (*auth-client-config*) created specifically for this purpose.

We so need to install:

```
sudo apt-get install libpam-ldap libnss-ldap auth-client-config
```

During setup *debconf* we are asked to insert the appropriate configuration, in our example:

```
LDAP server Uniform Resource Identifier => ldap:///localhost
Distinguished name of the search base: => dc=stenoit,dc=com
LDAP version to use: => <3>
Make local root Database admin: => <Yes>
Does the LDAP database require login? => <No>
LDAP account for root: => cn=admin,dc=stenoit,dc=com
LDAP root account password: => ldappwd
```

Now we open the file:

```
sudo nano /etc/ldap.conf
```

and we check that *debconf* has done its job. These parameters should be:

```
host 127.0.0.1
rootbinddn cn=admin,dc=stenoit,dc=com
base dc=stenoit,dc=com
```

There are two *ldap.conf* files, then copy the file you've just placed on the other by saving a copy:

```
sudo cp /etc/ldap/ldap.conf /etc/ldap/ldap.conf.bak
sudo cp /etc/ldap.conf /etc/ldap/ldap.conf
```

auth-client-config

This script, starting with a simple configuration profile, make the right customization on *nsswitch.conf* and on various PAM configuration files to set the correct authentication method.

It 's very convenient for those who want to deploy a configuration: once the profile is created with a simple command, you can set it correctly avoiding annoying typos.

We create, so, our profile:

```
sudo nano /etc/auth-client-config/profile.d/sbs_ldap
```

by entering:

```
[sbs_ldap]
nss_passwd=passwd: files ldap
nss_group=group: files ldap
nss_shadow=shadow: files ldap
nss_netgroup=netgroup: files ldap
pam_auth=auth        required    pam_env.so
        auth         sufficient  pam_unix.so likeauth nullok
        auth         required    pam_group.so use_first_pass
        auth         sufficient  pam_ldap.so use_first_pass
        auth         required    pam_deny.so
pam_account=account      sufficient   pam_unix.so
        account      sufficient  pam_ldap.so
        account      required    pam_deny.so
pam_password=password     sufficient   pam_unix.so nullok md5 shadow
        password     sufficient  pam_ldap.so use_first_pass
        password     required    pam_deny.so
pam_session=session      required     pam_limits.so
        session      required    pam_mkhomedir.so skel=/etc/skel/
        session      required    pam_unix.so
        session      optional    pam_ldap.so
```

The highlighted lines now wouldn't be necessary since they refer to *nsswitch* that we have previously already configured manually. However we can so understand how the script could operate also on it.

We are ready to configure PAM, we launch the command:

```
sudo auth-client-config -a -p sbs_ldap
```

Conclusions

The basic configuration of OpenLDAP of our server has ended and we should be able now to restart the service without errors:

```
sudo /etc/init.d/slapd restart
```

We can test it with:

```
ldapsearch -x
```

If we don't get errors but an empty LDIF list, it means that the service is up and running.

Now the LDAP database is still empty, we will start using and populating it in Chapter 8 when we will talk about File Server service.

Active Directory

In 1999, Microsoft, with the release of Windows 2000, introduced the *Active Directory* concept, a term which has always identified a set of network services adopted from their server operating systems, such as DNS, DHCP, LDAP, Kerberos, and mainly used as the database to store, in a hierarchical manner, all enterprise network services.

In this decade of life, given his considerable widespread use and versatility, *Active Directory* has become an almost universal reference point for user authentication services and management, to the point that today is really hard to find companies without such a service.

Ubuntu/Linux is no exception to this, and so we will see how to integrate it effectively by analyzing two alternative methods to authenticate local users using the Microsoft LDAP implementation.

Likewise Open

Likewise Open is a free software, released under the GPLv3 license, which allows simple integration between Linux and Microsoft Active Directory (AD). With this product you can join to the domain and then authenticate users using an external LDAP servers.

Installation

Ubuntu includes *Likewise Open standard* in its repository, then we could install it easily but, at the time of writing, the official package presents small bugs forcing us to use the repository development to get round this problem.

So we add the *ppa* Likewise repository by editing the file:

```
sudo nano /etc/apt/sources.list
```

and adding at the end the following lines:

```
deb http://ppa.launchpad.net/likewise-open/likewise-open-ppa/ubuntu lucid main
deb-src http://ppa.launchpad.net/likewise-open/likewise-open-ppa/ubuntu lucid main
```

We import the key to prevent installation errors and update the package list:

```
sudo apt-key adv --keyserver keyserver.ubuntu.com --recv-keys AAFDD5DB
sudo apt-get update
```

If problems arise, we can see the repository by accessing the site:

```
https://launchpad.net/likewise-open
```

Terminated this phase we can proceed with the installation itself with a simple:

```
sudo apt-get install likewise-open
```

If the file * /etc/resolv.conf* contains both our domain (*domain stenoit.com*) and DNS (*nameserver 192.168.20.2*) corresponding to the IP address of the Active Directory domain controller, there won't be any additional request and the installation will terminate immediately. Otherwise we should specify manually the domain name, the name of the *Kerberos* server of our *realm* and the administrative server name that should correspond to our Windows server with Active Directory without the domain part.

Here's an example of */etc/resolv.conf* :

```
domain stenoit.com
search stenoit.com
nameserver 192.168.20.2
```

Configuration

Likewise by default needs both the NETBIOS domain name and the user name to authenticate a user: this means that, for example *"projects1"* at logon must enter domain\username:

```
STENOIT\\projects1
```

It's pretty annoying, especially if we, as likely, have a single domain. To solve this problem we need to change the configuration of Likewise.

So, we edit the file:

```
sudo nano /etc/likewise-open/lsassd.reg
```

Set the following parameters in this way:

```
"AssumeDefaultDomain"=dword:00000001
"HomeDirTemplate"="%H/%D/%U"
```

AssumeDefaultDomain set to "1" means that now we can omit the domain name.

HomeDirTemplate indicates the path of the home for each user, that will be created automatically when you connect for he first time. For example home for user *"projects1"* becomes:

```
/home/STENOIT/projects1
```

Now we need to import changes:

```
sudo lwregshell import /etc/likewise-open/lsassd.reg
sudo lwsm refresh lsass
```

It is time to *join* our domain by typing the command:

```
sudo domainjoin-cli join stenoit.com Administrator
```

and the domain Administrator password.
Now reboot the system as proposed.

```
sudo reboot
```

After the first reboot a small detail has still to be fixed, that is to allow members of the Windows system group *"Domain Admins"* to manage our Linux server. To do this we make a simple change to *sudoers* file:

```
sudo visudo
```

by adding the following line:

```
%STENOIT\\domain^admins ALL=(ALL) ALL
```

Now even the domain user *"administrator"* will be allowed to use "sudo". To try, simply connect to the shell with the user and try to operate with the sudo command.

In conclusion we can say that *Likewise Open* is an excellent solution that greatly simplifies the integration of Linux with a Microsoft domain. However we remain disappointed by the fact that a LTS version of Ubuntu's repository does not contain the fully functional versions of the packages in question, which forces us to use an unofficial version of development in order to solve the problem.

Kerberos, Samba and Winbind

As seen above, then, we cannot ignore the fact that there is still the "old way" to integrate our server with Active Directory, a method that foresees the manual installation and configuration of the required software: *Kerberos* for authentication, *Samba and Winbind* for communication with ADS.

Installation

We install the needed packages:

```
sudo apt-get install samba winbind krb5-user libpam-krb5 krb5-
config libkdb5-4 libgssrpc4 smbclient
```

Configuration

Get the Kerberos ticket from the server:

```
sudo kinit Administrator@STENOIT.COM
```

Check and settle the Kerberos configuration file:

```
sudo nano /etc/krb5.conf
```

in particular, make sure that it contains:

```
[libdefaults]
        default_realm = STENOIT.COM

...

[realms]
        STENOIT.COM = {
                kdc = sbswin
                admin_server = sbswin
        }

...
```

where *sbswin* is our Windows AD server, and *STENOIT.COM* the domain name. To set correctly the parameters we can also use the command:

```
sudo dpkg-reconfigure krb5-config
```

Let's configure Samba, saving the default configuration file and creating a new one:

```
sudo mv /etc/samba/smb.conf /etc/samba/smb.conf.orig
sudo nano /etc/samba/smb.conf
```

writing inside as follows:

```
[global]
        server string = %h - SBS Server
        workgroup = STENOIT
        security = ads
        password server = sbswin.msg.it
        passdb backend = tdbsam
        winbind separator = +
        winbind refresh tickets = yes
        idmap backend = rid:MSG=70000-1000000
        idmap uid = 70000-1000000
        idmap gid = 70000-1000000
        winbind enum users = yes
        winbind enum groups = yes
        template homedir = /home/%D/%U
        template shell = /bin/bash
        client use spnego = yes
        client ntlmv2 auth = yes
        encrypt passwords = true
        winbind use default domain = yes
        restrict anonymous = 2
        realm = STENOIT.COM
        winbind enum groups = yes
        winbind enum users = yes
        syslog = 3
        log file = /var/log/samba/%m
```

```
max log size = 50
map acl inherit = Yes
username map = /etc/samba/smbusers
winbind cache time = 10
```

This series of parameters are the result of personal tests in order to obtain an optimal configuration. For further details, as usual, turn to the extensive literature that you find on the Internet.

Now let's check the resolution method of users and groups, ensuring that our:

```
sudo nano /etc/nsswitch.conf
```

contains:

```
passwd: compat winbind
group: compat winbind
shadow: compat
```

so even *winbind* is queried to find the user or group.

With *Likewise* on first log on the user's home was created automatically. To do so is made even now we have to edit the file:

```
sudo nano /etc/pam.d/common-session
```

by adding the following:

```
session required pam_mkhomedir.so umask=0022 skel=/etc/skel
```

To finish this part we stop and start the services:

```
sudo /etc/init.d/smbd stop
sudo /etc/init.d/smbd start
sudo /etc/init.d/winbind stop
sudo /etc/init.d/winbind stop
```

We can now *join* to the domain with the command:

```
sudo net ads join -U administrator
```

If everything went well you should see a message like this:

```
Using short domain name - STENOIT
Joined 'SBS' to realm 'stenoit.com'
```

If we get an error like *"DNS update failed!"* means that the Windows DNS does not accept unsecured dynamic updates. This does not affect the operation, we can manually add DNS table on your Linux server, but if we have to solve the issue, simply set the zone on the DNS server so that *"dynamic update"* must accept also unsecured update. See the Microsoft documentation about it.

We can check if *winbind* works with the command:

```
wbinfo -u
```

we should get the users list. With:

```
wbinfo -g
```

the list of groups. We try, also, to logon with a domain user on the bash shell, we should see us correctly on his home created at the first logon.
If there were problems re-sort all steps and try to restart services.

To finish here, as in the case of *Likewise Open*, we modify the sudoers file to allow domain administrators to use administrative commands via *sudo* from the shell of Linux servers.

```
sudo visudo
```

And add at the bottom:

```
%domain\ admins ALL=(ALL) ALL
```

That's all. We have seen two different ways (but very similar in depth) to integrate authentication of Ubuntu/Linux users with an external LDAP server, in this case *Microsoft Active Directory*.

Which one to use? I can say that *Likewise* has more configuration options (especially if you want to migrate to the commercial version) while the traditional method is much easier, more performant and therefore indicated if what you want to get is the simple user authentication on Active Directory, and little else.

5

DNS & DHCP Server

DNS services (*Domain Name System*), used to resolve host names to IP addresses and vice versa, and DHCP (*Dynamic Host Configuration Protocol*), which allows network devices to automatically receive the IP configuration needed to work, have become an essential service even in a small local network.

This chapter provides a simple but functional configuration to our needs, again without the pretense, of course, to be a complete guide to the services of this type.

Few years ago I was consulted to resolve a small but annoying issue. In a small peer to peer network with Windows and shared Internet access the *local network browsing was really slow*.

Why? The reason for this is attributable to the fact that the order in which Windows searches the hosts in the network is:

```
DNS -> files -> broadcast
```

So, to know the IP address of the neighbor host, first of all the Internet provider's DNS (the small network did not have a local DNS) was queried, and only after its obviously negative answer the local hosts file and the broadcast was used. The long response times were, so, a natural and obvious consequence. Now this kind of problems are easily solved with a simple router, but at that time were not so widespread, and this example is important to understand the importance of a DNS service also in small workgroups.

So, in this chapter, we will examine two alternative methods to provide our server of these essential services. We'll start with the simplest **dnsmasq** followed by the more standard and diffused coupled **bind & dhcpd**.

dnsmasq

For small networks, dnsmasq represents a very good solution: it is very easy to configure and integrate inside everything what we need: *Dynamic DNS*, *DHCP*, and *Caching*.

Let's see what we offer:

- ✔ The DNS configuration of computers behind the firewall is simple and does not depend on the provider's DNS.
- ✔ Clients that query the DNS when, for example, the Internet link is unavailable, receive time-out immediately, without unnecessary delays.
- ✔ Dnsmasq gets names from the */etc/hosts* file on the server: if the local machine name is found, we are immediately directed to the same without the need to maintain the hosts file on each machine.
- ✔ DHCP service supports static and dynamic DHCP leases and multiple IP ranges. The DHCP-configured machines are automatically placed in the DNS, and names can be specified in each machine or centrally by associating the name to the MAC address in the configuration file for dnsmasq.
- ✔ Dnsmasq caches Internet addresses (A records and AAAA records) and address-to-name mappings (PTR records), reducing the load on upstream servers and improving performance (especially on modem connections).
- ✔ Dnsmasq supports MX and SRV records and can be configured to return MX records for any or all local machines.

Installation

Install the package:

```
sudo apt-get install dnsmasq
```

Configuration

The configuration file is very well commented, but we start from a clean file by renaming the original for security and creating a new one:

```
sudo mv /etc/dnsmasq.conf /etc/dnsmasq.conf.backup
sudo nano /etc/dnsmasq.conf
```

insert this:

```
addn-hosts=/etc/dnshosts
no-hosts
server=/stenoit.com/192.168.20.1
domain=stenoit.com
```

```
interface=eth1
expand-hosts
dhcp-range=192.168.20.50,192.168.20.150,255.255.255.0,48h

# Router
dhcp-option=3,192.168.20.1

# set netbios-over-TCP/IP nameserver(s) aka WINS server(s)
dhcp-option=44,192.168.20.1

# netbios datagram distribution server
dhcp-option=45,192.168.20.1

dhcp-option=46,8 # netbios node type
dhcp-option=47 # empty netbios scope

# DNS
dhcp-option=6,192.168.20.1
dhcp-option=15,stenoit.com

dhcp-lease-max=500
mx-host=sbs.stenoit.com,50
mx-target=sbs.stenoit.com
localmx
log-queries
log-dhcp
strict-order
dhcp-authoritative
```

The DHCP automatically assigns an IP to devices in our network including in the range indicated by the *dhcp-range* parameter (from 192.168.20.50 to 192.168.20.150), together with the address of the default gateway, DNS, WINS and the other, specified in the various parameters *dhcp-options*. The additional parameters are numerous, to see those available we can run the command:

```
dnsmasq --help dhcp
```

If for some reason we must instead assign via DHCP a precise address to a network device, we need to know its *MAC address* (48-bit code assigned uniquely to each Ethernet network adapter in the world) and add this to the dnsmasq configuration file :

```
dhcp-host=00:1c:23:82:97:53,wks01,192.168.20.160
```

where the first parameter indicates the MAC address in hexadecimal, the second the name of the host on DNS and the third the IP address.

For any detailed explanations on individual parameters we refer to the basic but complete online help:

```
man dnsmasq
```

or the comments of its configuration file.

Now let's change again our file */etc/resolv.conf*:

```
sudo nano /etc/resolv.conf
```

that must contain the list of DNS servers that are queried, adding our *sbs* first and then the DNS provider which will cache (for us always OpenDNS):

```
search stenoit.com
nameserver 127.0.0.1
nameserver 208.67.222.222
nameserver 208.67.220.220
```

If we want to use static addresses just place them in the file */etc/dnshosts* (as specified by the parameter *addn-hosts*) in the usual form (without domain, which is provided by dnsmasq) that we use for the file */etc/hosts*. For example for another server with fixed IP:

```
192.168.20.2 myserver
```

dnsmasq will provide resolution of *myserver* or *myserver.stenoit.com* to all machines on the network.

We do not use the default */etc/hosts* file used by dnsmasq to prevent DNS to resolve the "private" names that I could put here, for example, *localhost*.

Edit the file:

```
sudo nano /etc/dnshosts
```

and add the following to have a basic resolution of addresses and names assigned to our server:

```
192.168.20.1 sbs mail stenoit.com
```

Finally, restart the service:

```
sudo /etc/init.d/dnsmasq restart
```

If we don't get error messages, our DNS/DHCP is ready. Computers on the network will be given an IP address, gateway, DNS, WINS and DNS registered on the table, so all other computers will be able to find them without worry about physical IP address.

Service testing

Let's try this:

```
ping stenoit.com
```

We should see:

```
PING stenoit.com (192.168.20.1) 56(84) bytes of data.
64 bytes from sbs.stenoit.com (192.168.20.1): icmp_seq=1 ttl=64 time=0.167 ms
```

Indicating that our DNS works and resolves domain names correctly.

If we need to control what addresses DHCP has released, we can do this by viewing the file:

```
sudo cat /var/lib/misc/dnsmasq.leases
```

If we do not have special needs we can safely stop here: *dnsmasq* works very well and, as we saw, is very simple to install and configure.

bind9 & dhcpd

If our network begins to become quite important, the *dnsmasq* solution begins to show its limitations and we have to use something more complete.

For example with *dnsmasq* we cannot handle multiple domains or install a backup DNS service if the primary one isn't reachable: given the importance of service this is intolerable in some more complex networks.

Let's see now how to solve the problem by installing and configuring the two packages representing practically the standards: Bind9 and DHCPD. Remember, *if we have installed dnsmasq, remove it before continuing!*

Bind9 installation

Install the packages:

```
sudo apt-get install bind9 dnsutils
```

DNS Caching

The simplest task that BIND can play is *"DNS caching"*, i.e. the simple local storage requests carried out by clients in our network.

By default BIND is already installed to act as a simple DNS caching. With this feature the performance in the resolution of Internet domain names in our network greatly improves, because BIND will "remember" your previous queries.

We set the configuration by defining the public DNS server to cache by editing the file:

```
sudo nano /etc/bind/named.conf.options
```

and defining in the section *"forwarders"* the provider's DNS (in this case are still those of OpenDNS):

```
forwarders {
        208.67.222.222;
        208.67.220.220;
        };
```

Also remember, if we hadn't already done so, to specify in the file */etc/resolv.-conf* our DNS:

```
search stenoit.com
nameserver 127.0.0.1
```

Restart the service:

```
sudo /etc/init.d/bind9 restart
```

and let's try a random domain:

```
dig google.com
```

we should also see the time taken by the query. For example:

```
;; Query time: 99 msec
```

Now by repeating again the same command as before, the time should be significantly reduced. For example:

```
;; Query time: 2 msec
```

demonstrating that the caching service is up and running.

BIND stores DNS information cache in RAM, not on the hard disk. It may not be a problem given that on modern machines this isn't usually lacking and that BIND deletes the oldest records periodically, but if we expect a high traffic it may be useful to flush cache occasionally with the command:

```
sudo rndc -s localhost flush
```

or set the maximum cache size with the parameter

```
max-cache-size
```

on the configuration file.

Master

But if we have internal IP addresses to be resolved into host names? In this case the service caching isn't enough and we must configure BIND as Master for our domain. So we will have a DNS that also resolves host names of the computers of our local network.

Suppose we have a small network with three servers and clients. A situation certainly implausible, but still functional to make a clear example:

Role	IP	Host name	Alias
DNS Server	192.168.20.1	sbs	dns
Mail Server	192.168.20.2	mail	pop3 smtp
Web Server	192.168.20.3	web	www
Workstation1	192.168.20.10	wks01	
Workstation2	192.168.20.11	wks02	

Workstation3	192.168.20.12	wks03

We see that the Mail server has two "alias" (canonical name, CNAME) and the Web server one (www). In this way we can have multiple names, simply refer to the same IP.

Zones

We define the "zone" whose management is delegated to our DNS, i.e. the domain and any sub-domains under our direct responsibility. For a more detailed explanation about the terminology (zone, alias, records type...) used by *Domain Name System* services, I always suggest to study this topic in depth using the enormous and free amount of documentation on the Internet, starting, for example, from the always excellent Wikipedia.

Ubuntu install a configuration file (*/etc/bind/named.conf*) that, except in special cases, does not need to be changed. It contains the basic configuration, such as defining default zones.

All our customizations, instead, will be made on a special secondary file:

```
sudo nano /etc/bind/named.conf.local
```

We add the definition zone for the correlation *IP->host* in our domain:

```
zone "stenoit.com" IN {
    type master;
    file "/etc/bind/zones/stenoit.com.db";
};
```

and its corresponding "reverse zones" indispensable for correlation host->IP:

```
zone "20.168.192.in-addr.arpa" {
    type master;
    file "/etc/bind/zones/20.168.192.in-addr.arpa";
};
```

The file names are completely arbitrary, but it is good practice to use self-describing names like those suggested here.

DNS records creation

Now that we have the two files available we can populate them with the appropriate values:

```
Host->IP file: /etc/bind/zones/stenoit.com.db
IP->Host file: /etc/bind/zones/20.168.192.in-addr.arpa
```

We create the first:

```
sudo mkdir /etc/bind/zones
sudo nano /etc/bind/zones/stenoit.com.db
```

by entering:

```
$ORIGIN .
$TTL 86400        ; 1 day
stenoit.com. IN SOA sbs.stenoit.com. admin.stenoit.com. (
    2010071001 ; numero di serie
    8H ; refresh
    4H ; retry
    4W ; expire
    1D ; minimum
)
```

1. The "." (dot) extra at the end of the host names is important because it indicates that the name written is complete. If omitted, *Bind appends the domain name to the string!*

2. the parameters set when DNS records expire etc.

3. *"admin.stenoit.com."* is not a host name, but the domain administrator e-mail address (*admin@stenoit.com*).

4. the serial number is important; to avoid undesirable consequences it must be always updated in every manual editing of table records. A good habit is to adopt a format *year-month-day-progressive (AAAAM-MGGPP)*.

Let's go on:

```
stenoit.com.         IN    NS          sbs.stenoit.com.
stenoit.com.         IN    MX    10    mail.stenoit.com.

$ORIGIN stenoit.com.
dns                  IN    CNAME       sbs.stenoit.com.
pop3                 IN    CNAME       mail.stenoit.com.
smtp                 IN    CNAME       mail.stenoit.com.
www                  IN    CNAME       web.stenoit.com.

localhost            IN    A           127.0.0.1

sbs                  IN    A           192.168.20.1
mail                 IN    A           192.168.20.2
web                  IN    A           192.168.20.3

wks01                IN    A           192.168.20.10
wks02                IN    A           192.168.20.11
wks03                IN    A           192.168.20.12
```

1. *NS* indicates that "sbs" is the Name Server of "stenoit.com"

2. *MX* means that *"mail"* is the mail server of the domain (10 is the priority, we can define multiple mail servers)

3. the *CNAME* define aliases. For example, *"web"* and *"www"* indicate the same host.

Now let's take care of "reverse":

```
sudo nano /etc/bind/zones/20.168.192.in-addr.arpa
```

Where, as now easily intuitable, we must define the reverse IP->Host equivalence.

```
$ORIGIN .
$TTL 86400      ; 1 day

20.168.192.in-addr.arpa IN SOA sbs.stenoit.com. admin.stenoit.com. (
     2010071001 ; serial
     8H ; refresh
     4H ; retry
     4W ; expire
     1D ; minimum
  )
             NS      sbs.stenoit.com.

$ORIGIN 20.168.192.in-addr.arpa.

1            PTR     sbs.stenoit.com.

2            PTR     mail.stenoit.com.
3            PTR     web.stenoit.com.

10           PTR     wks01.stenoit.com.
11           PTR     wks02.stenoit.com.
12           PTR     wks03.stenoit.com.
```

After having restart the service with:

```
sudo /etc/init.d/bind9 restart
```

we can test if it works. For example with:

```
dig web.stenoit.com
```

that, if there are problems, should give us the following output:

```
; <<>> DiG 9.7.0-P1 <<>> web.stenoit.com
;; global options: +cmd
;; Got answer:
;; ->>HEADER<<- opcode: QUERY, status: NOERROR, id: 4619
;; flags: qr aa rd ra; QUERY: 1, ANSWER: 1, AUTHORITY: 1, ADDI
TIONAL: 1

;; QUESTION SECTION:
;web.stenoit.com.              IN     A

;; ANSWER SECTION:
web.stenoit.com.        86400  IN     A      192.168.20.3
```

```
;; AUTHORITY SECTION:
stenoit.com.            86400   IN     NS      sbs.stenoit.com.

;; ADDITIONAL SECTION:
sbs.stenoit.com.        86400   IN     A       192.168.20.1

;; Query time: 0 msec
;; SERVER: 127.0.0.1#53(127.0.0.1)
;; WHEN: Tue Jul  6 16:04:09 2010
;; MSG SIZE  rcvd: 83
```

If there are problems check the log file, sometimes just a little thing in the wrong punctuation makes BIND become capricious and refuses to boot.

Otherwise our DNS is already up and running!

DHCPD

If the size of the network is important, manually assign IP addresses and update your DNS tables may become a heavy task to manage. The little *dnsmasq*, which included the DHCP functionality, did it automatically. Can't we do this also with bind?

Not directly, is the answer. We must rely on an independent software package called DHCPD that will assign IP addresses to those who will request it.

DHCPD installation

Let's start with the installation of the package:

```
sudo apt-get install dhcp3-server
```

when installation is finished, we receive an error message because we have not yet configured the service. Remedy by providing, for the moment, a basic configuration.

DHCPD configuration

Let's begin by defining the network interface on which the DHCP service will be active, in our case of course will be the internal one, named *"eth1"*:

```
sudo nano /etc/default/dhcp3-server
```

we put *"eth1"* in parameter *"INTERFACES"*:

```
# Defaults for dhcp initscript
# sourced by /etc/init.d/dhcp
# installed at /etc/default/dhcp3-server
# by the maintainer scripts
#
# This is a POSIX shell fragment
#
```

```
# On what interfaces should the DHCP server (dhcpd)
# serve DHCP requests?

# Separate multiple interfaces with spaces, e.g. "eth0 eth1".

INTERFACES="eth1"
```

Let's save the original configuration file (useful if we see additional parameters) and edit the new file:

```
sudo mv /etc/dhcp3/dhcpd.conf /etc/dhcp3/dhcpd.conf.orig
sudo nano /etc/dhcp3/dhcpd.conf
```

Let us remind you that what follows is only an example, the parameters are so many as the special cases. Refer to the official documentation for more information:

```
ddns-update-style none;

# options common to all networks, values "assigned" to all
option domain-name "stenoit.com";
option domain-name-servers 192.168.20.1;
option netbios-node-type 8;
option nntp-server 192.168.20.1;
option pop-server mail.stenoit.com;
option smtp-server mail.stenoit.com;

default-lease-time 600;
max-lease-time 7200;

# The DHCP server is the official one of our network
authoritative;

# Subnet declaration with range of addresses
# to assign and specific options

subnet 192.168.20.0 netmask 255.255.255.0 {
   range 192.168.20.100 192.168.20.200;
   # Default gateway
   option routers 192.168.20.1;
   option subnet-mask 255.255.255.0;
}

# The host wrk01 with specific MAC address is
# assigned this fixed IP address

host wrk01 {
   hardware ethernet 08:00:6F:82:92:5A;
   fixed-address 192.168.20.10;
}
```

We see that the subnet is defined, in range of addresses to assign, and other parameters explanatory enough, such as the fixed IP address to assign to a particular Host (wrk01) recognizable from the physical address (MAC Address) of its network adapter.

Now we can restart the service without errors, and we would have the DHCP running on the internal network.

```
sudo /etc/init.d/dhcp3-server start
```

Dynamic DNS

According to my opinion, we still have to make a final critical step: configure BIND and DHCPD to work together so that, when DHCPD assignes an IP address to a host, the record on BIND tables is also added or updated automatically.

Move zone files

First of all we have to move the zone files that we have created. Ubuntu 10.04 comes with the *AppArmor* security suite, whose standard profiles allow the reading only in default path */etc/bind/zones*.

Since we must update the tables, we need of course also the writing permission. To do this we need to move files in the folder specific areas covered by the security profiles of AppArmor, */var/lib/bind*.

In fact we could also change the standard AppArmor behavior by editing the file:

```
sudo nano /etc/apparmor.d/usr.sbin.named
```

but my advice is to keep the configuration standard proposed by the maintainer of the package.

Then move the files:

```
sudo mv /etc/bind/zones/* /var/lib/bind/
```

after that, we assign to "bind" user its ownership:

```
sudo chown bind.bind /var/lib/bind/*
```

Shared key

To ensure that the DHCP server is authorized to modify the DNS tables we need a "secret" key shared between them.

Create the key in this way:

```
sudo dnssec-keygen -r /dev/urandom -a HMAC-MD5 -b 128 -n USER DHCP_UPDATER
```

and display it:

```
sudo cat Kdhcp_updater.*.private|grep Key
```

in my case I got something like:

```
Key: fCbIn6MAtrwI9LYG3QvBgA==
```

Take note and continue with DNS.

DNS

Now proceed with the configuration for BIND. Edit the file:

```
sudo nano /etc/bind/named.conf.local
```

Adding the key we've just created and changing the file path in the definition of zones and specifying that the key DHCP_UPDATER is authorized to change the zone files:

```
key DHCP_UPDATER {
    algorithm HMAC-MD5.SIG-ALG.REG.INT;

    # This is the secret key.
    secret "fCbIn6MAtrwI9LYG3QvBgA==";

};

zone "stenoit.com" IN {
    type master;
    # Change the file path
    file "/var/lib/bind/stenoit.com.db";

    # DHCP_UPDATER key.
    allow-update { key DHCP_UPDATER; };
};

zone "20.168.192.in-addr.arpa"  {
    type master;
    # Change the file path

    file "/var/lib/bind/20.168.192.in-addr.arpa";

    # DHCP_UPDATER key.
    allow-update { key DHCP_UPDATER; };
};
```

DHCP

The last step is to configure DHCPD so that it updates the DNS tables using the generated key.

```
sudo nano /etc/dhcp3/dhcpd.conf
```

Here is the resulting configuration file. We pay attention to the bold lines showing the configuration parameters for dynamic update of the tables:

```
ddns-update-style interim;
ignore client-updates;
ddns-domainname "stenoit.com.";
ddns-rev-domainname "in-addr.arpa.";

# options common to all networks, values "assigned" to all
option domain-name "stenoit.com";
option domain-name-servers 192.168.20.1;
option netbios-node-type 8;
option nntp-server 192.168.20.1;
option pop-server mail.stenoit.com;
option smtp-server mail.stenoit.com;

default-lease-time 600;
max-lease-time 7200;

# The DHCP server is the official one of our network
authoritative;

key DHCP_UPDATER {
  algorithm HMAC-MD5.SIG-ALG.REG.INT;
  # La chiave condivisa
  secret "fCbIn6MAtrwI9LYG3QvBgA==";
};

zone stenoit.com. {
  primary 127.0.0.1;
  key DHCP_UPDATER;
}

zone 20.168.192.in-addr.arpa. {
  primary 127.0.0.1;
  key DHCP_UPDATER;
}

# Subnet declaration with range of addresses
# to assign and specific options
subnet 192.168.20.0 netmask 255.255.255.0 {
  range 192.168.20.100 192.168.20.200;
  #Default gateway
  option routers 192.168.20.1;
  option subnet-mask 255.255.255.0;
}

# The host wrk01 with specific MAC address is
# assigned this fixed IP address
host wrk01 {
  hardware ethernet 08:00:6F:82:92:5A;
  fixed-address 192.168.20.10;

}
```

Our configuration files contain the generated secret key. Let's change the permissions so that it isn't readable by others and remove the file that contains:

```
sudo chmod o-r /etc/bind/named.conf.local
sudo chmod o-r /etc/dhcp3/dhcpd.conf
sudo rm Kdhcp_updater.*
```

Finally we assign the configuration files to the correct owners and allow users who run services to interact together. We insert so the user "dhcpd" under "bind" group and "bind" user under "dhcpd" group:

```
sudo chown dhcpd.dhcpd /etc/dhcp3/dhcpd.conf
sudo chown bind.bind /etc/bind/*
sudo adduser dhcpd bind
sudo adduser bind dhcpd
```

Manual editing files

Now that the files are changed dynamically we must be careful if we need to add or change DNS records on the tables manually: Bind keeps journaling files (*.jnl) dynamically with changes that are not automatically synchronized with static files. This is a problem because if we are not careful our changes will be ignored.

But of course there is the solution: while in the past we had to stop the service, now thankfully we just have to use appropriately the **rndc** command to *"freeze"* the area affected, make changes, and then do a *"unfreeze"*.

Instead of doing it all manually here is a small bash script, called for the occasion *"dnsedit"*, that helps us to understand better.
We create the file:

```
sudo nano /usr/bin/dnsedit
```

and insert this code:

```
#!/bin/bash
echo Dynamic DNS Edit
echo ""
rndc freeze stenoit.com
rndc freeze 20.168.192.in-addr.arpa
nano /var/lib/bind/stenoit.com.db /var/lib/bind/20.168.192.in-addr.arpa
rndc unfreeze stenoit.com
rndc unfreeze 20.168.192.in-addr.arpa
echo ""
echo DNS editing terminated
```

Et voilà! After you have made executable the script with:

```
sudo chmod 755 /usr/bin/dnsedit
```

just type:

```
sudo dnsedit
```

The script seems to be very clear:

1. It puts "freeze" our zones
2. It edits with "nano" the necessary files, allowing us to add or modify our records
3. Once we exit, unfreeze zones

Warning! During editing with "nano" remind you to "increase" the zone serial in files, **otherwise our changes will not be reflected immediately!**

Zone file check

As already said it is easy to miss something in writing these configuration files. For this reason, before you start the service, we should check what we did with the appropriate *named-checkzone* command, specifying the name of the area and its files.

In our case:

```
sudo named-checkzone stenoit.com /var/lib/bind/stenoit.com.db
sudo named-checkzone 20.168.192.in-addr.arpa /var/lib/bind/20.168.192.in-addr.arpa
```

If it's all right we should not get any error message.
For example:

```
zone stenoit.com/IN: loaded serial 2010071001
OK
```

At the end restart services:

```
sudo /etc/init.d/bind9 restart
sudo /etc/init.d/dhcp3-server restart
```

Our professional DNS/DHCP service is up and running.

Active Directory

To set up an Active Directory domain the official recommendation from Microsoft is to abandon your old DNS Unix/Linux software and use the DNS server included in any version of Windows.

There are several Microsoft official documents about how to configure BIND to work with Active Directory, but they're all a bit outdated and cryptic to interpret accurately and they don't explain very well the procedure.

Relying on the Microsoft DNS service is a legitimate decision, but if we want to continue to rely on Ubuntu Linux for the management of this service, we see in this short paragraph how to solve the problem easily.

Fortunately, the recent implementation of Bind fully supports the dialog with a Domain Controller Active Directory, and the configuration process is exhausted in the mere implementation of Dynamic DNS service (DDNS) that we have just seen. The only change we must add to what we have seen, is to give permission to the Windows server to update the DNS tables.

Very briefly, edit the Bind configuration file:

```
sudo nano /etc/bind/named.conf.local
```

and let's change the two lines:

```
allow-update { key DHCP_UPDATER; };
```

like this:

```
allow-update { key DHCP_UPDATER; 192.168.20.2; };
```

where 192.168.20.2 is the IP address of the Windows server with Active Directory that will now be able to dynamically update the DNS zones.

That's all. After restarting the service we can perform a custom installation of Windows Server roles without the need to install its services otherwise necessary as DNS and DHCP.

6

Firewall Server

A firewall is a system designed to prevent unauthorized access to or from our private network (which may also be only the system itself). Can be implemented with dedicated hardware, software, or a combination of both. In the case we will treat, our little server will be the firewall of our company. This part is a bit complicated but we absolutely cannot ignore it: *we cannot live without a firewall!*

Firewalls are used especially to prevent that anyone outside of our network can access the local network, but also for the opposite reason: to prevent that our local users can access to unauthorized Internet services.

Each "packet" transmission that enters or exits from our network will be scanned by the firewall which, on the basis of the set security principles, will *allow* or *deny* the request.

Shorewall

Shoreline Firewall, more commonly known as Shorewall, is a high-level tool for configuring Netfilter, the Linux Kernel component that allows filtering and manipulation network data packages. The "rules" of the firewall are described using configuration files in text format relatively simple to understand and interpret by hiding the inherent complexity in Netfilter. Shorewall reads those configuration files and, with the help of standard *iptables* utility, configures it according to our needs.

Shorewall can be used on a dedicated firewall system, a multi-function gateway/router/server, or on a standalone GNU/Linux system. Is not a point-and-click and set-and-forget Linux firewall solution, it requires a minimum of networking knowledge. But its versatility and its excellent documentation will relieve our efforts.

Installation

We install Shorewall and its documentation with the command:

```
sudo apt-get install shorewall shorewall-doc
```

Configuration

Shorewall documentation includes the sample files for various popular cases, already almost ready for use.
We find them in:

```
/usr/share/doc/shorewall/examples
```

We have a classic server with two interfaces (*eth0* and *eth1*), so those that interest us are located at:

```
/usr/share/doc/shorewall/examples/two-interfaces
```

We copy them to /etc/shorewall:

```
sudo cp /usr/share/doc/shorewall/examples/two-interfaces/* /etc/shorewall/
```

Shorewall is a complex project but fortunately well documented. Here we are only going to see a simple summary of the configuration files that we are trying to understand the basics of how it works.

/etc/shorewall/interfaces

Here we define "aliases" of our network interfaces that then will be used in other configuration files. For us it will be like this:

```
#ZONE INTERFACE BCAST  OPTIONS
net   eth0       detect tcpflags,routefilter,nosmurfs,logmartians
loc   eth1       detect dhcp,tcpflags,nosmurfs,routeback
```

Then from that moment our *"internal"* adapter will be called '*loc*', the *"external"* one '*net* '. For the options please see the official guide, but let's pay particular attention to the *dhcp* parameter in the local interface that allows our server to provide IP addresses to the internal network.

/etc/shorewall/zones

Shorewall divides the networks of its competence in areas called *zones*. In the sample configuration *two-interfaces* the following names defined in the file */shorewall/zones are used*:

```
#ZONE TYPE OPTIONS IN OUT
## OPTIONS OPTIONS
fw firewall
net ipv4
loc ipv4
```

Note that Shorewall also assigns a zone to the firewall itself (FW). When the file */etc/shorewall/zones* is processed, the name of the firewall zone is stored in the shell variable *$FW* which can be used to refer to the firewall in its configuration files.

So we have three zones:

```
net -> external network (probably internet)
fw  -> the firewall itself
loc -> local network
```

We have to remember this, because when we define the rules to enable (with *ACCEPT*) or deny (with *REJECT* or *DROP*) traffic between interfaces we will always refer to zones. For example, do we want to connect to the server from the local network via ssh? We should create a separate rule by *loc->$fw*. Or do we want to access the Internet by the firewall itself? We should create a rule from *$fw->net*.

/etc/shorewall/policy

This file defines the default policy of our server. The file is well commented and helps us to understand the mechanism that Shorewall uses to configure the firewall. For example it contains:

```
#SOURCE DEST POLICY LOG LEVEL LIMIT:BURST
loc     net  ACCEPT
net     all  DROP   info

# THE FOLLOWING POLICY MUST BE LAST
all     all  REJECT info
```

The zone *"all"* does not exist in */etc/shorewall/zones*, it is used to refer to all zones. So by default our firewall will allow traffic from the internal network to the Internet (*loc net ACCEPT*) and blocks everything that comes from outside. The rules are applied in sequence, then it is good practice to close the file with the last one that rejects all if we had forgotten to set some filter (*all all REJECT*). The difference between DROP and REJECT is that the first simply ignores requests, and the second rejects and sends a notification.

To enable the firewall itself to access the Internet and local network PCs to access the services of the server, we have to add/modify these policy:

```
#SOURCE DEST POLICY LOG LEVEL LIMIT:BURST
$FW     net  ACCEPT
loc     $FW  ACCEPT
$FW     loc  ACCEPT
$FW     all  REJECT info
```

Now even our Firewall can access the Internet, and from the local network we can connect to the same (for example with SSH). From "net", instead, everything is refused. With the parameter "info" we indicate to Shorewall to write to the log file, in this case, the attempts at unauthorized access. Attention, as already mentioned, to leave as last the policy that blocks everything! (all all REJECT).

/etc/shorewall/rules

In this file are defined **exceptions** to the default policy defined in */etc/shorewall/policy*.

Now we have probably already understood how Shorewall works. In this file, however, it introduces a new concept.

This configuration file uses the so-called *macro*, default configurations that shorewall provides ready to use. We can see them in */usr/share/shorewall* and they are all those files that begin with "*macro.*".

For example look at *macro.DNS* and at *macro.HTTP* :

```
#ACTION SOURCE DEST PROTO DEST SOURCE ORIGINAL RATE USER/
## PORT PORT(S) DEST LIMIT GROUP
PARAM - - udp 53
PARAM - - tcp 53
#LAST LINE -- ADD YOUR ENTRIES BEFORE THIS ONE -- DO NOT REMOVE

#ACTION SOURCE DEST PROTO DEST SOURCE ORIGINAL RATE USER/
## PORT PORT(S) DEST LIMIT GROUP
PARAM - - tcp 80
#LAST LINE -- ADD YOUR ENTRIES BEFORE THIS ONE -- DO NOT REMOVE
```

We see that Shorewall defines for DNS the ports UDP and TCP 53 so in the configuration file we simply have to type:

```
#ACTION        SOURCE DEST PROTO DEST SOURCE
DNS(ACCEPT)    $FW    net
HTTP(ACCEPT)   loc    $FW
```

instead of:

```
#ACTION SOURCE DEST PROTO  DEST SOURCE
ACCEPT  $FW    net  tcp 53
ACCEPT  $FW    net  udp 53
ACCEPT  loc    $FW  tcp 80
```

Very easy and more readable. For example, let's block Ping from outside and we enable it within:

```
Ping(ACCEPT)   loc  $FW
Ping(REJECT)   net  $FW
```

IP Masquerading (SNAT)

Networks of the classes:

✔ 192.168.0.0
✔ 172.16.0.0 - 172.31.0.0
✔ 10.0.0.0

are reserved for local networks and they are never routed over the Internet.
To allow one of our users on the local network to connect to a host on the Internet, our firewall must act as a intermediator between the local and remote host. This process is called *"Network Address Translation (NAT)"*.

In GNU/Linux systems, this process is also known as *"IP Masquerading"* or sometimes it is also used the term *"Source Network Address Translation (SNAT)"*. Shorewall follows the following convention with Netfilter:

   ✔ **Masquerade** describes the situation when the Firewall automatically finds the address of the external interface
   ✔ **SNAT** when you explicitly specify the address

Masquerading and SNAT are both configured through the file */etc/shorewall/masq*. Normally Masquerading is used if the address of the external interface *eth0* has a dynamic IP address, SNAT if the IP address is static.

Here's our */etc/shorewall/masq* file:

```
#INTERFACE SOURCE            ADDRESS   PROTO   PORT(S) IPSEC   MARK
eth0       10.0.0.0/8,\
           169.254.0.0/16,\
           172.16.0.0/12,\
           192.168.0.0/16
```

In the column "SOURCE" the IP classes reserved to local networks are defined instead of a physical interface that may not be active when Shorewall is started (e.g. a VPN virtual device as we will see later).
In our specific case, since of course the local network interface is always active (*eth1*), we can safely specify herself in the second column:

```
#INTERFACE SOURCE ADDRESS
eth0       eth1
```

If the external address is static, we can place it in the third column of file */etc/shorewall/masq*. Will still work also ignoring this configuration, but the SNAT process (by specifying the address) should be more efficient.

```
#INTERFACE SOURCE ADDRESS
eth0       eth1   212.239.29.208
```

Of course the possibilities are numerous, such as allowing only certain hosts to navigate to Internet, or specify particular ports. We will see this in the last part of Chapter 10. For further details, let us consider the documentation of Shorewall, for now we will limit ourselves to this basic configuration.

Port Forwarding (DNAT)

Often it happens to "route" requests on firewall ports to a machine inside of our network. For example, suppose you have an internal web server on the machine with IP 192.168.20.10 that we want to achieve from the outside when someone directs the browser on port 8080 of the firewall. Just put in *etc/shorewall/rules*:

```
DNAT    net    loc:192.168.20.10:80    tcp    8080
```

Now requests to firewall port 8080 will be transferred to the internal system 192.168.20.10 on port 80.

Service startup

First we edit the primary configuration file for Shorewall:

```
sudo nano /etc/shorewall/shorewall.conf
```

by checking that these values are correct:

```
# Remember to put "Yes"!
STARTUP_ENABLED=Yes

# For gateway features
IP_FORWARDING=On

SUBSYSLOCK=/var/lock/shorewall
```

now we can enable the service. To do this edit the file:

```
sudo nano /etc/default/shorewall
```

and set:

```
startup=1
```

Shorewall can start in two ways, either with the classic one:

```
sudo /etc/init.d/shorewall start
```

or with its utility:

```
sudo shorewall start
```

The utility also has additional functionality such as:

```
sudo shorewall status
```

that shows us the status of the firewall. If there are problems during startup of the service we can discover the reason watching the appropriate log file:

```
/var/log/shorewall-init.log
```

The *shorewall* command has many options (*reset, save, show, ...*), by typing:

```
sudo shorewall --help
```

we can discover some of them useful, particularly when defining rules. For example, sometimes you make a flaw with Shorewall, but often you just need to analyze the log file:

```
sudo shorewall show log
```

while we try "something". We will see immediately the reasons on messages shown on the monitor.

Final considerations

As already said, this topic is *complex* and needs to be addressed *seriously and with competence*. Often an incorrect configuration of the firewall prevents the operation of other services or, worse still, it exposes to unnecessary risks.

Someone will not approve the solution adopted, i.e. every good network administrator knows that the corporate server shouldn't match the firewall. Fair. But this is beyond the scope of this guide. Who has knowledge of this argument will have no difficulties to do so by yourself, whether you opt for software or hardware dedicated solutions.

My last advice is (if possible) to disable Shorewall when you try a new service to prevent problems due to a bad packet filtering. For example if we install Samba and forget to allow traffic on its ports between the firewall and the LAN... needless to say that it won't work at all.

So beware: it is essential to know how to read the logs to identify problems!

7

LAMP Server

LAMP is an acronym that describes a platform for developing web applications that takes its name from the initials of software components that compose it.

The LAMP platform is one of the most widely used worldwide. Each of the applications from which it is composed, is designed for excellent operation in conjunction with the other. There are basically a couple of variations depending on which operating system you use. LAMP, Linux and WAMP, Windows. Of course we will discuss only the first instance. Here's our interpreters:

- ✔ L - Linux : operating system
- ✔ A - Apache : web server
- ✔ M - MySQL : database
- ✔ P - PHP (o Perl o Python) : Scripting language

I think I won't be far from true if I say that 95% of blogs in the world are based on this structure, if we add the WAMP instances and those on BSD platform, I believe we can achieve a Bulgarian share even more.

But why install a service like this in our Small Business? Because LAMP it is useful to run other software such as *Webmail, Proxy* and other applications with web interface that we need, like the console of *FAX services.*

Installation

The installation is very simple, there are many guides on how to do it, here's our interpretation, which corresponds to what we need:

```
sudo apt-get install apache2 apache2-doc php5 libapache2-mod-php5
php5-cli php5-cgi php5-gd php5-mysql php-pear mysql-server
```

When we are asked, we have to set the password for the MySQL admin user.

We have installed all the necessary adding also the Apache documentation, the support for PEAR (the largest online library of PHP modules) and the support for PHP scripts from the command line.

Configuration

We see the few things to configure for our small LAMP service:

Apache

We can change the default configuration file of Apache2 like this:

```
sudo nano /etc/apache2/apache2.conf
```

Here we can see that in addition to basic parameter (which we are not going to change), Apache adds many external *"Includes"* where we are going to configure specific aspects of our server.
In the various "include" for example we can see this:

```
# Include generic snippets of statements
Include /etc/apache2/conf.d/
```

that means that Apache includes all files in the directory, including apache-doc, which allows us to read with a browser the Apache documentation:

```
http://sbs.stenoit.com/manual
```

Let's do a test to include and publish also Shorewall documentation that we installed in the previous chapter:

```
sudo nano /etc/apache2/conf.d/shorewall-doc
```

And insert this:

```
Alias /shorewall /usr/share/doc/shorewall-doc/html/

<Directory "/usr/share/doc/shorewall-doc/html/">
    Options Indexes FollowSymlinks
    AllowOverride None
    Order allow,deny
    Allow from all
    AddDefaultCharset off
</Directory>
```

Restarting apache2 service:

```
sudo /etc/init.d/apache2 restart
```

or let it just read the new configuration.

```
sudo /etc/init.d/apache2 force-reload
```

Now by our browser we can access the Shorewall documentation so:

```
http://sbs.stenoit.com/shorewall
```

Apache is a modular software, it loads only the functionality needed for our installation. We can see in the directory:

```
/etc/apache2/mods-available
/etc/apache2/mods-enabled
```

available modules and those already enabled. For example if we wanted to install a CMS like Drupal, we should enable the *rewrite* module that is available but not enabled. To do this we use the command:

```
sudo a2enmod rewrite
```

To disable it we use:

```
sudo a2dismod rewrite
```

As last activity we edit the file:

```
sudo nano /etc/apache2/sites-available/default
```

that contains the configuration of our *default website*. We add at the bottom:

```
ServerName sbs.stenoit.com
```

and this parameter that indicates the correct Administrator's email:

```
ServerAdmin sbadmin@stenoit.com
```

For further information we refer to some specific Apache guide or its documentation that we can find online.

PHP

Apache is already configured to run PHP scripts and then we shouldn't do anything. We can check that the module is already enabled, with a simple "*ls*" command:

```
ls -al /etc/apache2/mods-enabled/ | grep php
```

we get:

```
lrwxrwxrwx 1 root root   27 2010-07-28 11:23 php5.conf -> ../mods-available/php5.conf
lrwxrwxrwx 1 root root   27 2010-07-28 11:23 php5.load -> ../mods-available/php5.load
```

if for some reason it weren't true we enable it with a simple:

```
sudo a2enmod php5
```

Let's take a further test by creating the file:

```
sudo nano /var/www/phpinfo.php
```

writing this:

```
<?php
  phpinfo();
?>
```

Now with our browser go to:

```
http://sbs.stenoit.com/phpinfo.php
```

and see the PHP configuration and its modules enabled.

MySQL

Even here there is nothing basic to do, the default configuration is already functional for our needs.

I just remember that by default MySQL accepts connections only from our server. If for some reason we wanted to access it from a PC on the network we must change the configuration:

```
sudo nano /etc/mysql/my.cnf
```

and set the bind-address directive on the internal interface:

```
bind-address          = 192.168.20.1
```

We can now also access the database server from a computer inside my network.

Warning: *no need to enable this option to use the LAMP services, in this case only our server will access MySQL through Apache/PHP and the default configuration is already correct.*

phpMyAdmin

We can test if it works by installing a couple of applications that are common components of a LAMP system. In addition, especially in the continuation of the Guide and in the day-to-day administration of the server, it will be a big help.

PhpMyAdmin is an open source PHP application that allows you to administer MySQL database through any browser.
We install it:

```
sudo apt-get install phpmyadmin
```

When we are asked which web server to set up, of course we choose apache2. Debconf will now create the file:

```
/etc/apache2/conf.d/phpmyadmin.conf
```

that will allow us to access to the management of our database server from this address:

```
http://sbs.stenoit.com/phpmyadmin
```

Before finishing the installation, Phpmyadmin asks us to create a configuration database. We accept the defaults by specifying the password for "root" that we set during the installation of MySQL, the same that then we will need to access the Web interface.

phpLDAPAdmin

The second application that we install is *phpLDAPAdmin*, a tool that will enable us to administer graphically through a common browser our LDAP tree. In particular we'll use it when we configure the server IM *Openfire* that we will meet in chapter 13.

We install it in this way:

```
sudo apt-get install phpldapadmin
```

and we configure it by editing its separate file to insert the correct values for our LDAP tree:

```
sudo nano /etc/phpldapadmin/config.php
```

and research and set the following parameters:

```
$servers->setValue('server','name','Stenoit LDAP Server');
$servers->setValue('server','base',array('dc=stenoit,dc=com'));
$servers->setValue('login','bind_id','cn=admin,dc=stenoit,dc=com');
```

We leave unchanged the remaining values.
Now we can access to the management interface of our LDAP server at this address:

```
http://sbs.stenoit.com/phpldapadmin
```

pressing "authenticate" and entering the ldap administrator password.

Conclusions

We stop here. Of course this isn't the most we can get, but for our purposes it is more than enough since that the HTTP server, as said, needs to us only how "appliance" for other services.

Pay attention to the firewall. MySQL should be accessible only (though I have not decided otherwise) from the server itself, so you don't have to open up its port (default is "3306") to the internal network. If we haven't fully enabled the internal traffic we must open the port "80" for http by adding to the file:

```
sudo /etc/shorewall/rules
```

the right directive:

```
HTTP(ACCEPT)           loc    $FW
```

and, if I want to be accessible from outside, also:

```
HTTP(ACCEPT)           net    $FW
```

8

File Server

This chapter is probably the most important. A file server in a company is certainly the primary, at least initially, purpose for which we install a server. In a company now no one can carries out daily tasks with no data sharing between users, and the simple peer to peer solutions have limitations that can't even consider here.

Before continuing, we summarize the basic concepts that must be clearly understood before proceeding with the implementation of the service itself.

Samba

With GNU/Linux we have several choices, but we only consider the Samba solution that allows us to interact well with clients of Microsoft Windows, that representing 98% of the business desktop market.

Samba is a large, complex project. The aim of the project is as simple as possible interoperability between the world of Microsoft Windows and Unix/Linux, also offering authentication services and file and printer sharing from any platform TCP/IP enabled. The original platforms were Unix and Linux, but today also other types of systems are successfully used.

What is this guide?

Risking to become monotonous we recall once again that *this is NOT a complete guide to Samba and OpenLDAP, or Samba and Active Directory.* In addition to what has been said here, it also assumes that we must already have a good understanding of how a network service based on a Windows Domain works.

Our goal here is to describe clearly a case of real implementation of a network that uses Microsoft Windows on users' desktops and Linux, Samba and Open-LDAP on the server side as an alternative of Microsoft server products. Since this is a project of a certain complexity, we must not overlook the fact that reading the excellent Samba official guide, freely downloadable from the project site, is more than just a tip: to do things without understanding them is a bad habit.

After that, as an alternative, we also see how we can integrate Ubuntu/Linux as a member server within an existing infrastructure based on Active Directory.

Is Samba Server better than Windows Server?

To be honest, in my opinion, the answer is NO. Samba is fantastic to "hide" the obvious differences between Windows and Linux/Posix, the result is not perfect, but since it is a product in constant and rapid evolution, these "imperfections" are becoming less discernible. It should be said that these "imperfections" do not refer to features within the services offered by Samba (these now have reached a very high degree of reliability, considering the fact that millions of PCS in the world use these services), but rather to the fact to persuade Windows clients that they are connecting to a "regular" Windows servers instead of Samba. Not all features have been implemented (such as nested groups and useful Group Policy), and then if we want to use Samba some advanced feature should be left aside.

Remember also that Samba CANNOT operate as ADS (Active Directory) Domain Controller (Windows Server 2000/2003/2008), but it can, as we shall see, effectively become a member as additional server. ADS Domain Controller functionality will be included in version 4 of Samba still under development.

Samba 3 can "emulate" a Windows NT4 Domain Controller even if with significant improvements in scalability largely due to the use of OpenLDAP as possible back-end (repository) for users, groups, and passwords. Of course, Windows 2000, Server 2003 and 2008 can effectively be integrated in a domain controlled by Samba 3 as member servers.

Why use Samba?

The reasons may be many.

- ✔ *Saving money.* Software license cost is *zero*. Caution, however, generally maintenance costs are roughly the same.
- ✔ *Security.* Also avoid criticizing the level of safety attained by Windows (depends of course who installs it), we cannot forget that Linux *is much less targeted by viruses, spyware* and malware.
- ✔ *Single Signon.* With OpenLDAP I can have a single repository of user/password for all Enterprise services (mail, network etc.). Chan-

ging password of a user is no longer a nightmare, each Desktop or Server, Windows or Linux, authenticates centrally in OpenLDAP tree.

Is it easier to use/administer Windows or Linux/Samba?

Here it would be difficult to find two people with the same opinion. Personally I can say that Windows and its Active Directory Services (ADS is a LDAP heavily customized by Microsoft for purpose) is an excellent product and to understand how to make a domain with it means chew disparate topics such as LDAP, DNS, DHCP, TCP/IP, KERBEROS, WINS, and all aspects related to a Microsoft network: the Primary Domain Controller (PDC), Backup Domain Controller (BDC), browsing the network, access control lists (ACLS), shares, Roaming Profiles, etc. In short, the argument is complex, and to climb through the installation of this type without know well these concepts is a bad idea.

And with Linux/Samba? Same thing, we have to know Linux, how to install and administer so at least basic, besides all the things which were spoken for Windows: LDAP, DNS, WINS, PDC, BDC, ACL, Roaming Profiles, etc.. Of course even with Samba we will find these concepts.

In the end the difference is that with Windows we have convenient (but in my opinion sometimes non-educational) GUI tools that do everything, with Linux we will have a mix between GUI tools and dear and old (but efficient) command line tools.

Do we have to replace our Windows servers with Linux/Samba?

Well, it depends. If we already have a functioning Windows ADS domain, it means that I have already invested in software licenses and miscellaneous costs, and replacing it with Samba is not leading to performed miraculous. If, as we will see later in this chapter, I must add a file server to the ADS domain, Samba can be a valid option.

Different if we should update some Windows NT servers, which obviously Microsoft no longer supports for years. Also in this case then, migrate to Samba can be a valid option.

Warning, if I have multiple servers we have to remember two important concepts:

- ✔ If the PDC is Windows all BDC must be Windows, additional member servers can be both Samba and Windows operating systems.
- ✔ If the PDC is Samba all BDC must be Samba servers, additional members can be both Samba and Windows operating systems.

Samba+OpenLDAP Domain Controller

Let's start so with the most interesting solution for us, the one that allows us to obtain an efficient File server and Domain Controller without the presence of Windows Server on your network.

Packages Installation

As a first step we have to install necessary packages.

Samba and LDAP tools

With Samba we install also the LDAP tools, which are a series of Perl scripts that allow us to manage users and groups Samba/Unix by saving data on LDAP tree instead of on canonical files */etc/passwd, /etc/shadow* file and */etc/group*. In short, they replace the standard Linux commands for user and group management.

```
sudo apt-get install samba samba-doc smbclient smbldap-tools
```

The scripts have been copied/installed in */usr/sbin* and the configuration files in */etc/smbldap-tools*.

The commands are in the form (for example to add a user):

```
sudo /usr/sbin/smbldap-useradd nomeutente
```

but don't try to do so now, lacking the necessary configuration we will get only an error.

Let's do something more: because of the inconvenient length of command and the frequency with which we will use them, we create symlinks in */bin*:

```
sudo ln -s /usr/sbin/smbldap-groupadd /bin/netgroupadd
sudo ln -s /usr/sbin/smbldap-groupdel /bin/netgroupdel
sudo ln -s /usr/sbin/smbldap-groupmod /bin/netgroupmod
sudo ln -s /usr/sbin/smbldap-groupshow /bin/netgroupshow
sudo ln -s /usr/sbin/smbldap-passwd /bin/netpasswd
sudo ln -s /usr/sbin/smbldap-useradd /bin/netuseradd
sudo ln -s /usr/sbin/smbldap-userdel /bin/netuserdel
sudo ln -s /usr/sbin/smbldap-userlist /bin/netuserlist
sudo ln -s /usr/sbin/smbldap-usermod /bin/netusermod
sudo ln -s /usr/sbin/smbldap-usershow /bin/netusershow
```

we can do this also with the equivalent (all on the same line):

```
for i in $(ls /usr/sbin/smbldap*) ;
do sudo ln -s $i /bin/net$(echo $i | cut -d"-" -f2);
done
```

the result does not change, we will be in */bin* simpler commands.

Now can type:

```
sudo netuseradd nomeutente
```

to get the same result as before.

Samba LDAP Schema

We need the *schema* file to apply to OpenLDAP to store the data that Samba need.

What is a schema file? LDAP is basically a database, the schema is the track record that describes, creates and declares the fields in the LDAP database. In the scheme of Samba there are fields for the user name, password, home, groups etc.. needed to store our data in the LDAP tree.

The file *samba.schema* we need is provided with the Samba documentation that we have installed before.

Copy it into the OpenLDAP directory :

```
sudo cp /usr/share/doc/samba-doc/examples/LDAP/samba.schema.gz /etc/ldap/schema/
sudo gzip -d /etc/ldap/schema/samba.schema.gz
```

Regarding the installation, we have finished.

OpenLDAP

We have already set basically OpenLDAP previously, now we see again its configuration to include what Samba needs.

Schema

First we need to enter information for Samba in *OpenLDAP Directory Information Tree* (DIT, see Chapter 4) by following step-by-step instructions, because Samba is not included with the LDIF file that we need. Let us begin with the creation of a conversion file:

```
nano /tmp/convert
```

by inserting the following:

```
include /etc/ldap/schema/core.schema
include /etc/ldap/schema/collective.schema
include /etc/ldap/schema/corba.schema
include /etc/ldap/schema/cosine.schema
include /etc/ldap/schema/duaconf.schema
include /etc/ldap/schema/dyngroup.schema
include /etc/ldap/schema/inetorgperson.schema
include /etc/ldap/schema/java.schema
include /etc/ldap/schema/misc.schema
include /etc/ldap/schema/nis.schema
include /etc/ldap/schema/openldap.schema
```

```
include /etc/ldap/schema/ppolicy.schema
include /etc/ldap/schema/samba.schema
```

Let's create a temporary directory:

```
mkdir /tmp/ldif
```

and with *slapcat* we execute the conversion (attention, **the command must be all in the same line!**):

```
slapcat -f /tmp/convert -F /tmp/ldif -n0 -s
    "cn={12}samba,cn=schema,cn=config" > /tmp/cn=samba.ldif
```

Now edit generated file:

```
nano /tmp/cn\=samba.ldif
```

and remove the *"{12}"* by these two lines, so that they become:

```
dn: cn=samba,cn=schema,cn=config
cn: samba
```

then we eliminate even the latest 7 rows at the bottom of the file that should be something like:

```
structuralObjectClass: olcSchemaConfig
entryUUID: e590d1a8-2e93-102f-98e0-2f490eb3e31a
creatorsName: cn=config
createTimestamp: 20100728130052Z
entryCSN: 20100728130052.689510Z#000000#000#000000
modifiersName: cn=config
modifyTimestamp: 20100728130052Z
```

Finally, we insert the information in the DIT:

```
sudo ldapadd -x -D cn=admin,cn=config -W -f /tmp/cn\=samba.ldif
```

typing the same password that we set in Chapter 4.

ACL

Now we set access rules to LDAP. First we create the LDIF file.

```
nano /tmp/smbacl.ldif
```

We insert into the file as follows (attention to parameters *olcAccess*: **must be onto a single line!**):

```
dn: olcDatabase={1}hdb,cn=config
changetype: modify
add: olcAccess
olcAccess: to dn.base="" by self write by * auth
olcAccess: to attrs=userPassword,sambaNTPassword,sambaLMPassword
  by dn="cn=admin,dc=stenoit,dc=com" write by anonymous auth
```

```
  by self write by * none
olcAccess: to * by * read by anonymous auth
```

Lets think about an important aspect: the rootdn *"cn=admin, dc=stenoit, dc=com"* have read/write access to the data, but very important is the access rule *"userPassword, sambaNTPassword, sambaLMPassword"* that in fact allows individual users to change their passwords directly from Windows with a *ctrl-alt-del*.

Load the file and put information in the DIT:

```
sudo ldapmodify -x -D cn=admin,cn=config -W -f /tmp/smbacl.ldif
```

Indexes

Now let's take care of useful indexes for faster searches. This stage is optional, but recommended. Once we create the necessary LDIF file:

```
nano /tmp/smbindex.ldif
```

with:

```
dn: olcDatabase={1}hdb,cn=config
changetype: modify
add: olcDbIndex
olcDbIndex: uidNumber eq
olcDbIndex: gidNumber eq
olcDbIndex: loginShell eq
olcDbIndex: memberUid eq,pres,sub
olcDbIndex: uniqueMember eq,pres
olcDbIndex: sambaSID eq
olcDbIndex: sambaPrimaryGroupSID eq
olcDbIndex: sambaGroupType eq
olcDbIndex: sambaSIDList eq
olcDbIndex: sambaDomainName eq
olcDbIndex: default sub
```

Once we upload the file which will create new indexes:

```
sudo ldapmodify -x -D cn=admin,cn=config -W -f /tmp/smbindex.ldif
```

Well, our tree is ready. We can, if desired, also check if everything works with the command:

```
ldapsearch -xLLL -D cn=admin,cn=config -x -b cn=config -W olcDatabase={1}hdb
```

that should show us active indexes and access rules that we have set.

LDAP Tools

LDAP tools are needed to manage users and groups, but first we must configure them to use them properly. First we stop the service, save the original configuration file and create a new one according to our needs:

```
sudo /etc/init.d/smbd stop
sudo mv /etc/samba/smb.conf /etc/smb.conf.backup
sudo nano /etc/samba/smb.conf
```

insert into the file:

```
[global]
        unix charset = LOCALE
        workgroup = STENOIT
        netbios name = SBS
        server string = %h PDC (%v)
        interfaces = eth1, lo
        bind interfaces only = Yes
        enable privileges = yes
        guest account = guest
        domain logons = Yes
        domain master = yes
        preferred master = Yes
        os level = 65
        wins support = Yes
        security = user
        ldap suffix = dc=stenoit,dc=com
        ldap user suffix = ou=Users
        ldap machine suffix = ou=Computers
        ldap group suffix = ou=Groups
        ldap idmap suffix = ou=Idmap
        ldap admin dn = cn=admin,dc=stenoit,dc=com
        idmap backend = ldap:ldap://sbs.stenoit.com
        idmap uid = 10000-20000
        idmap gid = 10000-20000
        ldap passwd sync = Yes
        #ldap ssl = start tls
        ldap ssl = no
```

As we can see at the moment (remember that the *Samba service is not running*) we provide only basic data, such as the domain (*workgroup = STENOIT*), the server name (*netbios name = SBS*), its role of *Domain Controller* (*domain logons = Yes*) and LDAP parameters.

As next step we take note of the *SID (Security Identifier)* of our domain. Remember that the SID, united then to *RID (Relative Identifier)*, is the name assigned by a Windows domain controller during the logon process used to identify an object (user or group for example).

By typing:

```
sudo net getlocalsid
```

we will obtain something like:

```
SID for domain SBS is: S-1-5-21-2656257307-2709483642-4015171607
```

Now we copy the sample *smbldap-tools* configuration file and then modify it to fit our needs:

```
sudo cp /usr/share/doc/smbldap-tools/examples/smbldap.conf.gz /etc/smbldap-tools/
sudo gzip -d /etc/smbldap-tools/smbldap.conf.gz
sudo cp /usr/share/doc/smbldap-tools/examples/smbldap_bind.conf /etc/smbldap-tools/
sudo nano /etc/smbldap-tools/smbldap.conf
```

scroll through the parameters we set them thus:

```
# The SID obtained with the above command
SID="S-1-5-21-2656257307-2709483642-4015171607"
sambaDomain="STENOIT"
#slaveLDAP="127.0.0.1"
masterLDAP="127.0.0.1"
ldapTLS="0"
#cafile="/etc/smbldap-tools/ca.pem"
#clientcert="/etc/smbldap-tools/smbldap-tools.iallanis.info.pem"
#clientkey="/etc/smbldap-tools/smbldap-tools.iallanis.info.key"
suffix="dc=stenoit,dc=com"
hash_encrypt="MD5"
userGecos="STENOIT Domain User"
defaultMaxPasswordAge="180"
userLoginShell="/bin/false"
userSmbHome=""
userProfile=""
userHomeDrive="K:"
userScript="%U.bat"
mailDomain="stenoit.com"
```

Others let them with default values. Save and then edit the file:

```
sudo nano /etc/smbldap-tools/smbldap_bind.conf
```

doing so it will become:

```
slaveDN="cn=admin,dc=stenoit,dc=com"
slavePw="ldappwd"
masterDN="cn=admin,dc=stenoit,dc=com"
masterPw="ldappwd"
```

Remember again that *"ldappwd"* is the LDAP administration password that we decided in Chapter 4.

When we have finished this step we protect files from accidental changes (*smbldap.conf*) and also from prying eyes (*smbldap_bind.conf*):

```
sudo chmod 0644 /etc/smbldap-tools/smbldap.conf
sudo chmod 0600 /etc/smbldap-tools/smbldap_bind.conf
```

Now we just have to say to Samba the password to use for accessing LDAP:

```
sudo smbpasswd -w ldappwd
```

If we get a response like this:

```
Setting stored password for "cn=admin,dc=stenoit,dc=com" in secrets.tdb
```

Means that until now everything has gone right, and we can continue.

Populating LDAP

In order to work correctly Samba needs several default groups and two users: *administrator* and *guest*. In addition, if we want to add computers to the domain automatically (from Windows machines), there must be a user with *uid=0* to use for this operation. This user can be a root user (to be added by hand) or the same Administrator renaming it the UID.

The latter one is the chosen solution in this configuration, so we have a user *Administrator who is Administrator for Samba and root for the "domain" UNIX.*

The *ldap-tools* provide a convenient command that does this: *smbldap-populate*. We execute it well with these parameters (the command **on single line**):

```
sudo /usr/sbin/smbldap-populate -a administrator -u 5001 -g 5001 -r 5001
        -b guest -l 5000
```

at the end we are asked the password of "Administrator", we have used the same of root user (if enabled) to avoid confusion. We should see something like this:

```
Populating LDAP directory for domain STENOIT (S-1-5-21-3546531168-
556325961-4035814821)
(using builtin directory structure)

entry dc=stenoit,dc=com already exist.
adding new entry: ou=Users,dc=stenoit,dc=com
adding new entry: ou=Groups,dc=stenoit,dc=com
adding new entry: ou=Computers,dc=stenoit,dc=com
adding new entry: ou=Idmap,dc=stenoit,dc=com
adding new entry: uid=administrator,ou=Users,dc=stenoit,dc=com
adding new entry: uid=guest,ou=Users,dc=stenoit,dc=com
adding new entry: cn=Domain Admins,ou=Groups,dc=stenoit,dc=com
adding new entry: cn=Domain Users,ou=Groups,dc=stenoit,dc=com
adding new entry: cn=Domain Guests,ou=Groups,dc=stenoit,dc=com
adding new entry: cn=Domain Computers,ou=Groups,dc=stenoit,dc=com
adding new entry: cn=Administrators,ou=Groups,dc=stenoit,dc=com
adding new entry: cn=Account Operators,ou=Groups,dc=stenoit,dc=com
adding new entry: cn=Print Operators,ou=Groups,dc=stenoit,dc=com
adding new entry: cn=Backup Operators,ou=Groups,dc=stenoit,dc=com
adding new entry: cn=Replicators,ou=Groups,dc=stenoit,dc=com
adding new entry: sambaDomainName=STENOIT,dc=stenoit,dc=com

Please provide a password for the domain administrator:
```

As we see, *smbldap-populate has* created users and groups present in a default installation of Windows Server. Now, to see if everything works we try to create a user *"user1"*:

```
sudo netuseradd -a -m user1
```

give it a password:

```
sudo netpasswd user1
```

and check if the user now exists:

```
sudo getent passwd
```

We should get the list of users including:

```
administrator:x:0:0:Netbios Domain Administrator:/home/administrator:/bin/false
guest:x:5000:65534:guest:/nonexistent:/bin/sh
user1:x:5001:513:SMBDOM Domain User:/home/user1:/bin/false
```

to know the options available we type *"netuseradd"* without parameters and let's take a look. In this example, the *"-a"* switch creates both the UNIX user and Samba, and *"-m"* creates the home user (*/home/user1*).

Users and Groups

It's almost time to start Samba, but first we need to plan what we're going to share and how to set the access to the file system (ACL). What we are proposing here is just one example, the cases can be numerous, but this is still a good starting point.

We define and create a set of groups and users and assign them also a private share:

Group	Description
sales	users of Sales Department
projects	users of Projects Department
Domain Users	All domain users

Domain Users has already been created with *smbldap-populate*. Each new user is assigned automatically to this group.

Creating groups

```
sudo netgroupadd -a Sales
sudo netgroupadd -a Projects
```

Creating users

```
sudo netuseradd -a -m sales1
sudo netpasswd sales1
sudo netuseradd -a -m projects1
sudo netpasswd projects1
```

if we did everything correctly, we should not see errors, check with:

```
sudo getent passwd
```

at the bottom you should see the newly created users:

```
sales1:x:5002:513:STENOIT Domain User:/home/sales1:/bin/false
projects1:x:5003:513:STENOIT Domain User:/home/projects1:/bin/false
```

Please note: as we can see every user is not granted shell access (*/bin/false*). If we wanted to give this privilege simply edit the user (for example *projects1*) so:

```
sudo netusermod -s /bin/bash projects1
```

Assign users to groups

```
sudo netgroupmod -m sales1 Sales
sudo netgroupmod -m projects1 Projects
```

Also here we can control with:

```
sudo getent group
```

and get something like:

```
Sales:*:5001:sales1
Projects:*:5002:projects1
```

net* commands are in */bin*, it is useful to familiarize yourself with them to administer users and groups.

Server as a member of Active Directory

If our network already has a Microsoft Active Directory domain controller, we can evaluate a useful alternative: we can configure Samba to use its authentication features to create an additional file server.

But why should we use Samba + Linux if we already have a Windows File Server? What advantage do you get? At least three:

1. Greater scalability. Maybe for small installations it doesn't affect very much, but it helps to know that the performance of Samba degrades much more slowly than Windows.
2. File System. Or maybe do we still prefer to use a file system that is fragmented?
3. Backup. Only with a native file system of Linux we can use the great Snapshot Backup technique shown in Chapter 12.

Packages installation

We have already seen in Chapter 4 how to make that users are authenticated by an external ADS server and how to join to the domain. This stage, so, should have been already successfully completed.

Now, if in Chapter 4 we have chosen the solution *Kerberos, Samba and Winbind* we do not need any additional package, if instead we have chosen the solution *Likewise Open* we must add the following:

```
sudo apt-get install samba samba-doc smbclient winbind
```

In any case we do not need *smbldap-tool* package.

Users and Groups

All users and groups management is performed using the tools provided in Windows environment, then locally on Ubuntu server you don't need to do anything.

Shares

Let's see now the organization of shares. What we will do here of course should not be considered a universal rule, but only a possible idea on how to approach this topic.

Let's see, so, what we are going to share, putting everything (except the home directory) in */samba*:

Share	Path	Description
public	/samba/public	Public share. Contains a folder for each group (see below)
netlogon	/samba/netlogon	Necessary system share on a domain controller. Contains user logon scripts. Not necessary if our server is a member of an Active Directory domain.
profiles	/samba/profiles	System share. Necessary if we use *Windows Roaming profiles*. I can use them even in case of Active Directory environment if the Samba server is the primary server.
rootdir	/samba	Share for backup purposes. Also contains the symlink to most important files on the server
apps	/samba/apps	Applications share. Read-only
homes	/home	Personal home folders for users. In the case of Active Directory, instead, we set in */home/STENOIT*

public

This is the main share, instead of creating one for each group we put everything into a public and "Let's play" then with permissions on folders. To understand better:

/samba/public	
/samba/public/sales	Folder for "Sales" group
/samba/public/projects	Folder for "Projects" group
/samba/public/common	Folder for all users ("Domain Users")

When we work with many groups could be quite tedious and confusing do separate shares (L:\, M:\, N:\, and so on). A user who is a member of several groups would be with many different mappings that exhausts in short the alphabet. So instead we will have a unique mapping (L:\) and everyone will see the sub folders that will access. Much more tidy and comfortable.

In our case, so, we will map only one unit *L:* on share *"public"* and users in group *"Sales"* will see *L:\COMMON* and *L:\SALES*, while users in group *"Projects"* will see only *L:\COMMON* and *L:\PROJECTS*. None (except members of the group "Domain Admins") can create files or folders in the root of network drive *L:*.

Let's start by creating the structure:

```
sudo mkdir -p /samba/public
sudo mkdir -p /samba/public/sales
sudo mkdir -p /samba/public/projects
sudo mkdir -p /samba/public/common
```

and we fix the permissions and ownership:

```
sudo chmod 770 /samba/public/sales
sudo chgrp Sales /samba/public/sales
sudo chmod 770 /samba/public/projects
sudo chgrp Projects /samba/public/projects
sudo chmod 770 /samba/public/common
sudo chgrp "Domain Users" /samba/public/common
```

then we control what we did:

```
ls -al /samba/public
```

seeing something like this:

```
drwxr-xr-x 5 root root         4096 2010-07-28 16:53 .
drwxr-xr-x 3 root root         4096 2010-07-28 16:53 ..
drwxrwx--- 2 root Sales        4096 2010-07-28 16:53 sales
drwxrwx--- 2 root Domain Users 4096 2010-07-28 16:53 common
drwxrwx--- 2 root Projects     4096 2010-07-28 16:53 projects
```

setuid

Now that we have set the permissions of the folders we are faced with an unexpected problem. When users create new files or folders, these shares are flagged with *user=UserCreator* and *group=DefaultUserGroup*. The default group is *"Domain Users"*, then all new files are set up with this group. So the new files created in "sales" are theoretically visible to the users of the "Projects", as they are also members of the group "Domain Users". In this case they are protected by the permissions on the folder itself but it couldn't be so in another case. In addition, the user *"Administrator"* has the default group

"Domain Admins", so every file created/copied/restored by the administrator is not accessible to "normal" users. Undoubtedly a nuisance to reset every time the permissions on the files by hand manipulated by the administrator.

To solve this problem the *UNIX SETUID flag is of great help*. We enable the flag on the group in this way:

```
sudo chmod g+s /samba/public/sales
sudo chmod g+s /samba/public/projects
sudo chmod g+s /samba/public/common
```

If now we check with *"ls -al"* command, we should see that the permission triplet group is changed from *rwx* to *rws* indicating that the setuid flag is enabled. What does this mean? Simply this trick makes that every file that is created in the folders *will have, as a group owner, the group folder and not the user.* So every file, for example, created on *"sales"* will have as a group owner *"Sales"* which is the group that owns the folder.

Enjoy! Now we can use also "Administrator" to restore or create files that will be accessible to normal users.

netlogon & profiles

These are two system shares, necessary when you configure a *domain controller*. In *netlogon* there will be the users logon scripts (that we'll see how to create them immediately in a dynamic way), while in *profiles* the user profiles will be there if we wanted to use Microsoft Roaming Profiles.

Create folders and set their permissions:

```
sudo mkdir /samba/netlogon
sudo mkdir /samba/profiles
sudo chmod 777 /samba/profiles
```

rootdir

This is a share of "convenience" accessible only to the administrator. We create a system folder with *symlinks* to folders or files that then we could save via Samba share from another PC to make a fast backup.

```
sudo ln -s /home /samba/home
```

In this way when the user *administrator* will access the share "rootdir", it can see and manipulate all home users

```
sudo mkdir /samba/system
sudo ln -s /etc /samba/system/etc
sudo ln -s /var/lib/ldap /samba/system/ldap
```

Now the Administrator finds in folder "system" even the server configuration files and the database users/groups of OpenLDAP. Very handy, and I could also add other links without having to invent "exotic" shares.

apps

In this share we place network shared software programs. Only "Administrator" can write to the folder, other users can only read and execute files. We create the folder and set the permissions:

```
sudo mkdir /samba/apps
sudo chmod 750 /samba/apps
sudo chgrp "Domain Users" /samba/apps
sudo chmod g+s /samba/apps
```

homes

This share is automatically created by Samba. The home user will be mapped to K: and it will be private to each user.

We should be there. Now we are ready to complete the configuration of Samba and to start the service.

smb.conf

We return, then, on the Samba configuration file. We configure it well and start the service. We also see a brief explanation of the main parameters applied to our smb.conf

Global parameters

Edit the Samba configuration file:

```
sudo nano /etc/samba/smb.conf
```

and now we see what to put inside.

In the *[global]* section we see the General parameters of the service, we will focus only on the most significant. We distinguish the two cases proposed: *OpenLDAP + Samba Domain Controller* and *Member Server in an Active Directory domain.*

Samba+OpenLDAP Domain Controller

Domain name:

```
workgroup = STENOIT
```

Server name:

```
netbios name = SBS
```

Samba listens only on specified interfaces, the eth0 which is outward towards the Internet of course is not served.

```
interfaces = eth1, lo
bind interfaces only = Yes
```

We tell Samba that the repository of users, groups and password is the LDAP server:

```
passdb backend = ldapsam:ldap://sbs.stenoit.com
```

Order in which workstation names are resolved. Broadcast last.

```
name resolve order = wins host dns bcast
```

Script invoked by Samba when, from *Windows,* we try the specified tasks. This allows us to use the windows tools to manage users and groups, as well as performing the *join* to the domain.

```
add user script = /bin/netuseradd -a -m '%u'
delete user script = /bin/netuserdel '%u'
add group script = /bin/netgroupadd -a -p '%g'
delete group script = /bin/netgroupdel '%g'
add user to group script = /bin/netgroupmod -m '%u' '%g'
delete user from group script = /bin/netgroupmod -x '%u' '%g'
set primary group script = /bin/netusermod -g '%g' '%u'
add machine script = /bin/netuseradd -w '%u'
```

Logon script executed by users when they connect. *%U* is transformed in the username. For example the user "projects1" runs (if any) the script named "projects1.bat" located in *netlogon share.*

```
logon script = %U.bat
```

We don't want *Roaming Profiles*, and then we put *null* in these parameters. Let us note that the parameters *"userSmbHome"* and *"userProfile"* specified in */etc/smbldap-tools/smbldap.conf* take precedence over these!

```
logon path =
logon home =
```

Our server is a *domain controller*

```
domain logons = Yes
```

We elect our server at highest authority making it become *"Master Browser"* for the segment of our network.

```
domain master = yes
preferred master = Yes
os level = 65
```

Our server is also WINS server:

```
wins support = Yes
```

LDAP tree parameters that Samba connects. In this way we indicate to Samba where to find users, groups, computers, and the user name to use to connect himself (admin).
Password we stored earlier with the command *"smbpasswd -w"*.

```
ldap suffix = dc=stenoit,dc=com
ldap user suffix = ou=Users
ldap machine suffix = ou=Computers
ldap group suffix = ou=Groups
ldap idmap suffix = ou=Idmap
ldap admin dn = cn=admin,dc=stenoit,dc=com
idmap backend = ldap:ldap://sbs.stenoit.com
idmap uid = 10000-20000
idmap gid = 10000-20000
ldap passwd sync = Yes
ldap ssl = no
```

The authentication type to use (VERY IMPORTANT!).

```
security = user
```

Here is anyway the section *[global]* proposed in its entirety, useful if we want to analyze by ourselves also parameters not explained.

```
[global]
        workgroup = STENOIT
        netbios name = SBS
        server string = %h PDC (%v)
        interfaces = eth1, lo
        bind interfaces only = Yes
        passdb backend = ldapsam:ldap://sbs.stenoit.com
        enable privileges = yes
        log level = 0
        log file = /var/log/samba/%m
        max log size = 50
        smb ports = 139 445
        hide dot files = yes
        name resolve order = wins host dns bcast
        time server = Yes
        guest account = guest
        show add printer wizard = No
        add user script = /bin/netuseradd -a -m '%u'
        delete user script = /bin/netuserdel '%u'
        add group script = /bin/netgroupadd -a -p '%g'
        delete group script = /bin/netgroupdel '%g'
        add user to group script = /bin/netgroupmod -m '%u' '%g'
        delete user from group script = /bin/netgroupmod -x '%u' '%g'
        # Disabilitare quando a fare il join al dominio è un Windows NT
         set primary group script = /bin/netusermod -g '%g' '%u'
        add machine script = /bin/netuseradd -w '%u'
        logon script = %U.bat
        # Profili Roaming
        #logon path = \\%L\profiles\%U
        logon path =
        logon home =
        logon drive = K:
```

```
domain logons = Yes
domain master = yes
preferred master = Yes
os level = 65
wins support = Yes
# LDAP
ldap suffix = dc=stenoit,dc=com
ldap user suffix = ou=Users
ldap machine suffix = ou=Computers
ldap group suffix = ou=Groups
ldap idmap suffix = ou=Idmap
ldap admin dn = cn=admin,dc=stenoit,dc=com
idmap backend = ldap:ldap://sbs.stenoit.com
idmap uid = 10000-20000
idmap gid = 10000-20000
ldap passwd sync = Yes
#ldap ssl = start tls
ldap ssl = no
map acl inherit = Yes
#printing = cups
lock directory = /var/lock/samba
winbind use default domain = yes
winbind enum users = yes
winbind enum groups = yes
security = user
template shell = /bin/false
```

Server as a member of Active Directory

We've already seen the parameters in Chapter 4. We see roughly what they mean.

Domain name:

```
workgroup = STENOIT
```

We tell Samba that the manager of users, groups and password is the domain controller Active Directory named *sbswin*:

```
password server = sbswin.stenoit.com
```

Winbind parameters for the mapping of users:

```
winbind separator = ^
winbind refresh tickets = yes
idmap backend = rid:STENOIT=70000-1000000
idmap uid = 70000-1000000
idmap gid = 70000-1000000
winbind enum users = yes
winbind enum groups = yes
winbind cache time = 10
winbind use default domain = yes
```

The *root* user, and group *"Domain Admins"* can administer the server:

```
admin users = root @"STENOIT^Domain Admins"
```

Administrative domain of Kerberos authentication:

```
realm = STENOIT.COM
```

But especially the type of authentication to use:

```
security = ads
```

Also here, as before, we show the section [global] proposed in its full version:

```
[global]
        server string = %h - File Server
        workgroup = STENOIT
        security = ads
        password server = sbswin.stenoit.com
        passdb backend = tdbsam
        winbind separator = ^
        winbind refresh tickets = yes
        idmap backend = rid:STENOIT=70000-1000000
        idmap uid = 70000-1000000
        idmap gid = 70000-1000000
        winbind enum users = yes
        winbind enum groups = yes
        winbind cache time = 10
        template homedir = /home/%D/%U
        template shell = /bin/bash
        client use spnego = yes
        client ntlmv2 auth = yes
        encrypt passwords = true
        winbind use default domain = yes
        restrict anonymous = 2
        realm = STENOIT.COM
        winbind enum groups = yes
        winbind enum users = yes
        log file = /var/log/samba/%m
        max log size = 50
        map acl inherit = Yes
        printing = bsd
        print command = lpr -r -P'%p' %s
        lpq command = lpq -P'%p'
        lprm command = lprm -P'%p' %j
        unix charset = LOCALE
        username map = /etc/samba/smbusers
        admin users = root @"STENOIT^Domain Admins"
        log level = 0
        read raw = yes
        write raw = yes
        kernel oplocks = yes
        max xmit = 65535
        dead time = 15
        getwd cache = yes
        socket options = TCP_NODELAY
        delete readonly = yes
        oplocks = yes
```

As mentioned earlier, this is just one example, but fully functional in real installations and developed over time.

Now we move to the section *"shares"*.

Shares

We've already seen before which shares we will create, let's see how it has been translated to the configuration file. We don't analyze all, but only those that have some significant parameter to explain. We can find the full version of the *smb.conf* at the end.

public

Share name and path:

```
comment = "L: - Public Folder"
path = /samba/public
```

Writable:

```
writeable = yes
```

We see it in network *browsing*.

```
browseable = Yes
```

Hide files and folders that the user cannot read. This is useful, in this share a user will see only what they need.

```
hide unreadable = Yes
```

This set of parameters leading the way in which files and folders are created by users over the network. We have listed the ones that work well for most cases.

```
directory mask = 0775
create mask = 0775
force create mode = 0775
force directory mode = 6775
security mask = 0777
force security mode = 0
directory security mask = 0777
force directory security mode = 0
```

The *vfs objects* are a useful Samba "plugin". In this case we use the recycle object to implement a network Recycle Bin. Deleted files won't be deleted immediately, but they will be copied to a hidden folder called ".trash/*username*". Then we make a script called *"purge"* to empty the bins every so often. The additional parameters need us to tell Samba not to save temporary and backup files and not to apply *versioning* to MS Office files (create problems with the his "Automatic Save").

```
vfs objects = recycle
recycle:repository = .trash/%U
recycle:keeptree = yes
recycle:touch = yes
```

```
recycle:versions= yes
recycle:exclude = *.tmp *.bak ~$*
recycle:exclude_dir = /tmp /temp /cache
recycle:noversions = *.doc *.xls *.ppt
```

netlogon

This part should be ignored if you are installing an Active Directory member server. If our server is the Domain Controller this "service" sharing is essential for handling user logon script.

Meanwhile we hide from browsing the network.

```
browseable = No
```

When the user logs on to the share (and all users in a domain do it) it runs */etc/samba/logon.pl* passing of parameters, like the user name that invoked the script, the group, time etc..

This small Perl script creates the user's logon script immediately according to the rules defined within it. For example creates *"sales1.bat"* for user *"sales1"*. We may omit this parameter and create by hand the script, but so it is much more convenient.

```
root preexec = /etc/samba/logon.pl "%U" "%G" "%L" "%T" "%m" "%a"
```

And now we see how this *logon.pl is done.* Edit:

```
sudo nano /etc/samba/logon.pl
```

and insert:

```perl
#!/usr/bin/perl
#
open LOG, ">>/var/log/samba/netlogon.log";
print LOG "$ARGV[3] - User $ARGV[0] connected to $ARGV[2]\n";
close LOG;

# Users list for every share
$APPS    ="-projects1-projects2-";
$NOLOGON ="-administrator-";
$DELMAP  ="-winnt-win2k-win2k3-winxp-";
$ADMIN   ="administrator";

# Script generation - begin
open LOGON, ">/samba/netlogon/$ARGV[0].bat";
print LOGON "\@ECHO OFF\r\n";
print LOGON "ECHO SBS logon script\r\n";
print LOGON "ECHO.\r\n";

# Synchronize time with the server
print LOGON "NET TIME \\\\SBS /SET /YES\r\n";

# If PC platform in list $DELMAP clears old maps
if (index($DELMAP,"-".lc($ARGV[5])."-") >=0)
  {
        print LOGON "NET USE * /DEL /YES\r\n";
  }
```

```
# Exit if user in list $NOLOGON otherwise apply common maps
if (index($NOLOGON,"-".lc($ARGV[0])."-") == -1)
  {
    # Drive L: (PUBLIC)
    print LOGON "NET USE L: \\\SBS\\public /YES\r\n";
    # Drive K: (HOME)
    print LOGON "NET USE K: \\\SBS\\$ARGV[0] /YES\r\n";

    # Drive X: (APPS)
    if (index($APPS,"-".lc($ARGV[0])."-") >=0)
      {
        print LOGON "NET USE X: \\\SBS\\apps /YES\r\n";
      }
  }
# Close file.
close LOGON;
```

We can see that we *condition* scripting on the basis of variables in the head. For example, only the users list specified in *$APPS* variable (projects1 and projects2 separated with "-") will have the "X:" mapping, and users listed in *$NOLOGON* (administrator) will not have any script.

This Perl script can be modified and extended easily by following this sample schema, and has the advantage to simplify the management of the logon script.

Do we want that also the user *"sales1"* maps the "X:" to *\\SBS\apps*? Just add it in the list *$APPS* and the next time you will connect to the server it will have its script updated immediately. In addition we will have a log file in */var/log/samba/netlogon.log* that informs us of the time users logon.

Similarly, using the parameter *"root postexec"*, we can create a script that, for example, write to log the time that a user has disconnected.

Be careful, it is clear that the parameters *"root preexec"* (and *"root postexec"* that runs during the "logoff") are not a prerogative of netlogon share. They can be used with any share to do "something" when you connect (and/or disconnection from it).

Remember to make it executable:

```
sudo chmod +x /etc/samba/logon.pl
```

And, finally, here is the complete configuration file, with regard to the shares, by *looking through* and study. We can, for example, notice that we have managed the Recycle Bin also on home and authorized only members of the group "Domain Admins" to access the "service" share *rootdir*.

In the case of "Active Directory Member" we omit these parameters, the configuration in the *[global]* section is sufficient. Remember also that the sharing *[netlogon]* is necessary just in case our server is a Domain Controller.

```
[public]
        comment = "L: - User public folder"
        path = /samba/public
        writeable = yes
```

```
        browseable = Yes
        hide unreadable = Yes
        directory mask = 0775
        create mask = 0775
        force create mode = 0775
        force directory mode = 6775
        security mask = 0777
        force security mode = 0
        directory security mask = 0777
        force directory security mode = 0
        #inherit acls = yes
        #inherit permissions = yes
        vfs objects = recycle
        recycle:repository = .cestino/%U
        recycle:keeptree = yes
        recycle:touch = yes
        recycle:versions= yes
        recycle:exclude = *.tmp *.bak ~$*
        recycle:exclude_dir = /tmp /temp /cache
        recycle:noversions = *.doc *.xls *.ppt

[homes]
        comment = "K: - Private folder - %U"
        writeable = yes
        create mask = 0700
        directory mask = 0775
        browseable = No
        force user = %U
        vfs objects = recycle
        recycle:repository = .trash
        recycle:keeptree = yes
        recycle:touch = yes
        recycle:versions= yes
        recycle:exclude = *.tmp *.bak ~$*
        recycle:exclude_dir = /tmp /temp /cache
        recycle:noversions = *.doc *.xls *.ppte_dir = /tmp /temp /cache
        recycle:noversions = *.doc *.xls *.ppt

[rootdir]
        comment = Service folder
        path = /samba
        writeable = yes
        browseable = yes
        directory mask = 0770
        create mask = 0775
        force create mode = 0775
        force directory mode = 6775
        security mask = 0777
        force security mode = 0
        directory security mask = 0777

        # Only for "Domain Controller" configuration
          admin users = Administrator
          valid users = "@Domain Admins"

        force create mode = 0644
        force directory mode = 6775

[apps]
        comment = "X: - Apps"
        path = /samba/apps
        writeable = yes
```

```
        browseable = Yes
        directory mask = 0770
        create mask = 0775
        security mask = 0777
        force security mode = 0
        directory security mask = 0777
        force directory security mode = 0
        hide unreadable = Yes
        force create mode = 0775
        force directory mode = 6775

# Only for "Domain Controller" configuration
[netlogon]
        comment = Network Logon Service
        path = /samba/netlogon
        guest ok = Yes
        locking = No
        browseable = No
        root preexec = /etc/samba/logon.pl "%U" "%G" "%L" "%T" "%m" "%a"
        #root postexec = /etc/samba/logoff.pl "%U" "%G" "%L" "%T"


[profiles]
        comment = Profile Share
        path = /samba/profiles
        writeable = yes
        create mask = 0660
        directory mask = 0770
        profile acls = Yes
        browsable = No
```

Start the service

```
sudo /etc/init.d/smbd start
```

Now that we have finally started Samba, we can do the *join* to our domain, we check that functions and create a couple of useful bash script for system main-tenance.

Join to domain

The "join" is done as follows:

```
sudo net rpc join -S SBS -U administrator
```

after entering the password you should see the message:

```
Joined domain STENOIT.
```

At this stage Samba has created the account for our workstations in its LDAP backend server in the format *"machinename$"*. Let's see if it is true with the *getent* command:

```
sudo getent passwd
```

At the end we should see our server:

```
sbs$:*:5004:515:Computer:/dev/null:/bin/false
```

Test operation

Let's use Samba commands, so we are sure that Itself responds to our requests:

```
sudo pdbedit -L
```

A "Member Server" should show us only local users, while a "Domain Controller" the complete users list, like this:

```
Administrator:0:Administrator
guest:5000:guest
sales1:5001:sales1
projects1:5002:projects1
sbs$:5004:Computer
```

and now we also shares:

```
sudo smbclient -L localhost -U administrator
```

after the password we should see something like:

```
Domain=[STENOIT] OS=[Unix] Server=[Samba 3.4.7]
        Sharename       Type      Comment
        ---------       ----      -------
        public          Disk      L: - User Public Folder
        rootdir         Disk      Service folder
        apps            Disk      X: - Apps
        IPC$            IPC       IPC Service (sbs PDC (3.4.7))
        Administrator   Disk      K: - Private folder- administrator

Domain=[STENOIT] OS=[Unix] Server=[Samba 3.4.7]


        Server              Comment
        ---------           -------
        SBS                 sbs PDC (3.4.7)


        Workgroup           Master
        ---------           -------
        STENOIT             SBS
```

In the case of "Member Server" will see references to ADS.

Enjoy! Our Domain Controller is ready to welcome our Windows workstation (and Linux), while our Member Server is ready to work in tandem with the Active Directory Domain Controller.

Maintenance Scripts

Now here's a couple of useful maintenance scripts in the administration of our File Server.

purge

Previously we have enabled the Samba plugin to manage the Recycle Bin of your server: when a user deletes a file, in fact Samba moves it to the folder *"./trash/username"* that we have defined.

It seems obvious that we cannot leave them there forever, but we need to *purge* trash folders from time to time to keep our system clean from junk.

Who knew Novell Netware purge command will also remember that it played very well this feature, unfortunately we do not have anything like that, and we have to manage with a bash script.

We create the script:

```
sudo nano /bin/purge
```

like this:

```
#!/bin/bash
# purge
# Empty trash user and system
# by steno 2005-2007

# Check parameters
if [ $# = 0 ]
 then
   echo "use: purge {all|<username>}"
   exit;
 else
  if [ $1 = 'all' ]
   then
    DIR=`ls /home -F | awk '/\/$/ {sub( /\/$/,""); print}'`;
   else
    DIR=$1;
  fi;
fi;

# Empty users private trash
for user in $DIR; do
  if [ -e /home/$user/.trash ];
    then
    X="`(cd /home/$user/.trash ; echo *)`";
    if [ ! "$X" = "*" ] ; then
              echo "Empty trash user <$user>";
              rm /home/$user/.trash/* -r;
    else
              echo "Personal trash of <$user> is empty";
    fi;
  fi;
done;

# Empty global trash "public" share
DIR=`ls /samba/public/.trash -F | awk '/\/$/ {sub( /\/$/,""); print}'`;

for user in $DIR; do
 X="`(cd /samba/public/.trash/$user ; echo *)`";
 if [ ! "$X" = "*" ] ; then
  echo "Empty global trash of user <$user>" ;
  rm /samba/public/.trash/$user -R;
 else
```

```
    echo "Global trash of <$user> is empty";
    fi

done;
```

The script is divided into two parts, one dealing with bins of every single *"/home/user"*, the second bins of *"public"* share.
We make the script executable:

```
sudo chmod 755 /bin/purge
```

and we create the global Recycle Bin giving correct permissions to the folder:

```
sudo mkdir /samba/public/.trash
sudo chmod 770 /samba/public/.trash
sudo chgrp "Domain Users" /samba/public/.trash
```

Now run the command *"purge all"* from the shell to empty all the bins, *"purge sales1"* or the single user sales1 bin. We also take into consideration the possibility to schedule with *crontab* to automatically start at "dusk."

setchown

This script is less used, but in some cases it is very useful. What is its job? Simple, it corrects the permissions on files and directories of *home users*.

Sometimes it happens, as administrator, to restore, copy or move files from one folder to another user and then having to manually work with *chown* and *chmod* to fix all the correct permissions and ownership. The script *"setchown"* does it automatically browsing through all the home users (with parameter *"all"*) to correct permissions and ownership. We create the file:

```
sudo nano /bin/setchown
```

like this:

```
#!/bin/bash
# setchown
# correct file permissions and ownership
# exclude from process the home listed in var "exclude"

exclude="sbsadmin ftp";

# Check parameters
if [ $# = 0 ]
  then
    echo "use: setchown {all|<username>}"
    exit;
else
  if [ $1 = 'all' ]
    then
      DIR=`ls /home -F | awk '/\/$/ {sub( /\/$/,""); print}'`;
    else
      DIR=$1;
  fi;
fi;
```

```
for user in $DIR; do
    mask=${exclude#*$user};
    if [ "$mask" = "$exclude" ]
    then
      chown $user /home/$user -R
      chmod 700 /home/$user
      echo "Permissions fixed in /home/$user";
    fi
done
```

Also here we see that we can execute *"setchown all"* for all homes or *"setchown sales1"* for single home.

Do not forget to make the script executable:

```
sudo chmod +x /bin/setchown
```

In variable *"$exclude"* we can enter the list of folders in the home that we do not want to process.

Firewall

If we have not granted free access from local computers to server on */etc/shorewall/policy,* we need to fix the firewall, changing the *rules* file:

```
sudo nano /etc/shorewall/rules
```

adding the new rules:

```
SMB(ACCEPT) $FW loc
SMB(ACCEPT) loc $FW
```

To restart the service we use the *shorewall* command, so let's see if we made mistakes:

```
sudo shorewall restart
```

Real life

For simple domains with a few users we could be ok in this way, but the reality is quite different from the theory and now we see why with a simple example.

In a real work setting the configuration is rarely so straightforward and simple and it can often happen a particular case that we cannot manage.

Here's an example that proves once again how far away can be the border between theory and practice.

We tell a story.

Windows users

We all have used or still use Windows. This operating system is the engine by 92-94% (depending on studies) of the PC on this planet. Impossible not to keep it in consideration.

A typical user of this operating system (and for typical I mean those who use it for work or play without technical knowledge computing) never had to do with *"access rights"* and *"permissions on files or activities"* of the computer. They probably don't even know that they exist, since 99% of PCs with Windows work with *"Administrator"* or equivalent user. (Often if you subtract this rule even certain software don't work, then I candidly admit that well *I work as Administrator in Windows*).

But when they discover that they exist, however, they can start to make fanciful requests:

"I want to see Jack files that can see those of John but cannot delete those of Lucy. Right? "

They come to us "Network Administrator" and begin to bombard us with requests like this.

Without going on a paradox, we present a very frequent case and not at all unjustified, and see if we can solve it with Samba.

Here is, for example, what might be required:

"Jack and John manage the product data sheets. I want to save their drawings on "L:\products" and Lucy and Mary could see them or send them to customers without change or cancel them."

Well, I would say, a reasonable request. Enough, however, to disconcert us. Let's see why.

Let's go to work!

So, we have the share *"public"* (that our users call "L:\"), we create users, the folder "products" and a group "product" that as members has Jack and John. If we are working with a member server in Active Directory to create users and groups, we obviously have to use the tools provided by Windows, or let us do it with the commands provided by *smbldap* as we have seen:

```
sudo netuseradd -a -m Jack
sudo netpasswd Jack
sudo netuseradd -a -m John
sudo netpasswd John
sudo netgroupadd -a Products
sudo netgroupmod -m Jack,John Products
```

We also create the necessary folders and assign permissions:

```
sudo mkdir /samba/public/products
sudo chmod 770 /samba/public/products
sudo chgrp Prodotti /samba/public/products
sudo chmod g+s /samba/public/products
```

Now Jack and John have *L:\products* on which can read and write freely without having in any way changed the configuration of Samba, we have only acted on users groups and permissions on the file system.

Go ahead. Now we create the users Mary and Lucy and their group "Products-RO" (Read Only) always using the appropriate tools:

```
sudo netuseradd -a -m Lucy
sudo netpasswd Lucy
sudo netuseradd -a -m Mary
sudo netpasswd Mary
sudo netgroupadd -a Products-RO
sudo netgroupmod -m Lucy,Mary Products-RO
```

And now, *what should we do?*

1. Let's change permissions putting *"755"* on */samba/public/products*, so the *"others"* can read but not write to it. Wrong. In this way, even users in the *"Sales"* group, which have nothing to do, can read it.
2. We use smb.conf parameters *"Read List"* and *"Write List"*. Wrong. These parameters affect all *"public"* share and override those in the file system. Lucy and Mary, in this case, could not even write *L:\COMMON*.
3. We make a share *"products"* separate and unrelated from *"public"*. OK, it works, but we don't like it. If for every case we have to make a separate share, soon we exhaust the letters of the alphabet to map and our *SMB.conf* becomes a book. And then they asked us *"L:\products"*, wouldn't we want to disappoint them? With Windows it is done in two seconds...

Samba has nothing to do with this limitation. Samba based its services on the file system that has found (ext3 or ext4 in our case) and he does everything possible to "mask" them, but in this case it can do nothing.

We just discovered the great limitation of the triplet mechanism *"rwxrwxrwx"* typical of Unix and Linux File Systems. They almost make us smile when compared to the granularity of permissions that we can reach with NTFS.

They are inadequate. Completely inadequate. Fortunately, someone noticed it before us, and quite a few years ago.

POSIX ACL

The solution to our problem goes through an extension of permission management called **POSIX ACL**. It is still a draft, not easy to understand and manage but perfectly working on Linux.

Install the package:

```
sudo apt-get install acl
```

we edit our */etc/fstab*:

```
sudo nano /etc/fstab
```

and we enable them by specifying the flag *"acl"* in mount of our file system, which will have a complicated name behind a string "UUID". For example:

```
# /dev/sda1
UUID=5ffc3239-8b00-45b9-a65c... / ext4 relatime,errors=remount-ro 0 1
```

becomes:

```
# /dev/sda1
UUID=5ffc3239-8b00-45b9-a65c... / ext4 acl,relatime,errors=remount-ro 0 1
```

Reboot the server or simply remount the file system with:

```
sudo mount -o remount /
```

and we're okay. Extensions are enabled.

setfacl & getfacl

These are our two new friends, *"setfacl"* to set the extended permissions and *"getfacl"* to see them. We don't explain how they work in detail Posix ACLs, there are those who have already done it optimally, on the Internet you can easily find much documentation on this topic.

Now this is our situation:

```
drwxrws---  2 root Products    4096 21 dec 15:46 products
```

We show it with:

```
sudo getfacl /samba/public/products
```

achieving this, we have not yet activated any extension and then correspond to normal flags that we all know:

```
# file: samba/public/products
# owner: root
# group: Products
user::rwx
```

```
group::rwx
other::---
```

Now we set our desired permissions to the group "products-RO":

```
sudo setfacl -d -m group:Products-RO:r-x /samba/public/products
sudo setfacl -m group:Products-RO:r-x /samba/public/products
```

We show it again:

```
sudo getfacl /samba/public/products
```

and this time I get:

```
# file: products
# owner: root
# group: Products
user::rwx
group::rwx
group:Products-RO:r-x
mask::rwx
other::---
default:user::rwx
default:group::rwx
default:group:Products-RO:r-x
default:mask::rwx
default:other::---
```

Well. We granted read permissions for the group "Permissions-RO" setting them as default. Problem solved!

If now we check the situation again with "*ls -al*" see this:

```
drwxrws---+  2 root Products     4096 21 dec 15:46 products
```

The "+" sign at the end indicates that in folder "products" the POSIX ACL extensions are active.

What should we learn from this example? This last part is mainly to understand how even simple problems can sometimes make us give up if we do not a have basic knowledge. Be careful at cases like this, there are many and for some of them you can't even find a solution.

Samba PDF manuals have more than 1200 pages and no writing at all. The funny part is that reading and studying them, we understand well how Windows works better than many other people.

Disk Quotas

Before ending we analyze another interesting but often neglected aspect, especially in medium to large networks: the management of "*Journaled Disk Quotas.*"

This function can be assigned to users or groups, a disk space that can not overcome. This, as for Posix ACLs, involves the file system and you can only set to the entire volume mounted, and not on single directory or share.

For example if we wanted to set different disk quotas for the "home" (K:) and the "public" (L:) they should reside on separate file systems. Samba will use these settings and then each user/group will see the mounted volume of the maximum size that can be used.

In addition, shares may not only control the number of bytes consumed, but also the number of *inodes*: this means we can actually set the maximum number of files that a user/group is allowed to create.

Concepts

Before implementing the *"Disk Quotas"*, it is best to first understand how they actually work and how they are applied. We have three basic concepts to understand, *"Hard Limit"*, *"Soft Limit"* and *"Grace Period"*. Let's see what they mean and how to set them later.

Hard Limit

The *"hard limit"* defines the maximum number of disk space (or the maximum number of files) that the user or group can use (or create). When the limit is reached is not given more space and an error is generated.

Soft Limit

The *"soft limit"* defines the maximum amount of disk space (or the maximum number of files) that can be used (or created). However, unlike the *"hard limit"* as above, the limit can be exceeded for some time. This period is called *"grace period"*.

Grace Period

The *"grace period"* is, as we have seen, the time during which the *"soft limit"* can be overcome. The *"grace period"* can be expressed in seconds, minutes, hours, days, weeks or months, giving us great flexibility to define precisely how long our users may exceed the limit set by us.

Installation and configuration

First install the needed packages:

```
sudo apt-get install quota quotatool
```

We open again, as with the ACL, our */etc/fstab*:

```
sudo nano /etc/fstab
```

and enable the *"Disk Quotas"* (with journaling) by specifying the appropriate flag in the mount of our file system, for example:

```
# /dev/sda1
UUID=5ffc3239-8b00-45b9-a65c... / ext4 acl,errors=remount-ro 0 1
```

becomes **(all on one line)** :

```
# /dev/sda1
UUID=5ffc3239-8b00-45b9-a65c... / ext4 acl,usrjquota=aquota.user,
    grpjquota=aquota.group,jqfmt=vfsv0,errors=remount-ro 0 1
```

Let's create the necessary files and remount the file system (remember that in this example, we are always talking about the root file system "/"):

```
sudo touch /aquota.user /aquota.group
sudo chmod 600 /aquota.*
sudo mount -o remount /
```

At this time, our file system is able to work with quotas, even if it is not yet ready to support them. To overcome this we must first run the command *quotacheck* who will examine the file system and create the table on the current use for each user (the file created earlier, *aquota.user*) and for each group (the file aquota.group). At the end of the process we enabled their management with the command *quotaon*:

```
sudo quotacheck -avugm
sudo quotaon -avug
```

That's all. Now *"Journaled Disk Quotas"* extensions are up and running.

Quota assignment

The mechanism with which quotas are assigned is relatively simple. We must use the command *edquota* both for the users and groups, keeping in mind that the quotas assigned to a specific user take precedence over those of the group of which he is a member.

Edquota, like visudo and crontab, uses the system editor to modify the settings. For example with command:

```
sudo edquota -u projects1
```

system editor is opened and we should see something like this:

```
Disk quotas for user tecnico1 (uid 5003):
 Filesystem blocks    soft    hard inodes    soft     hard
 /dev/sda1      20       0       0      5       0        0
```

The value *"0"* means that there is no limit. With the editor we can change these values, for example in this manner:

```
Disk quotas for user tecnico1 (uid 5003):
 Filesystem  blocks     soft      hard  inodes     soft      hard
 /dev/sda1      20 5000000  7000000       5        0         0
```

we define that the user "projects1" has a soft limit of 5GB and a hard limit of 7GB. The limit will be visible, such as maximum size of the disk, even if the user connects to a Windows share of the server file system.

Similarly we can set quotas at the group level, although there is a complication in the fact that, in Samba, shall be implemented only quotas assigned to the user's primary group that is, as defined by parameter *defaultUserGid* in the file */etc/smbldap-tools/smbldap.conf*, the group *"Domain Users"* (gid = 513).

```
# Default User (POSIX and Samba) GID
defaultUserGid="513"
```

So, in order to effectively assign a quota that includes all members of a group other than "Domain Users", I must first change the user's primary group. Here's an example with the users "projects1" and "projects2" members of the "Projects" group, to which we assign a quota. We start with finding the GID of the group that we are interested in:

```
sudo netgroupshow projects
```

we'll get something like this:

```
dn: cn=Projects,ou=Groups,dc=stenoit,dc=com
objectClass: top,posixGroup,sambaGroupMapping
 cn: Projects
 gidNumber: 5003
 sambaSID: S-1-5-21-3546531168-556325961-4035814821-11007
 sambaGroupType: 2
 displayName: Projects
 memberUid: prjects1,projects2
```

So we set with "5003" the primary group for users:

```
sudo netusermod project1 -g 5003
sudo netusermod project2 -g 5003
```

At this point we can check to be sure that the command has worked:

```
sudo netusershow projects1
```

and I should see, among the others, the parameter correctly set:

```
gidNumber: 5003
```

Now we are ready to set quotas for the group "projects" with the command:

```
edquota -g projects
```

we will show the usual editor with values almost identical to what was seen for the individual user.

The relative ease with which you manage the quotas will not be fooled: the difficult thing is not planning how to assign it, but how large it should be. A simplistic approach might be to divide the volume available to users, for example, with 100GB and 10 users could be assigned 10GB as "hard limit" to every user.

A variation on this could be the technique called *"over-commit"*, which is to assign more space to each user's thinking that, statistically, they do not all at the same time: we could then assign, for example, a "soft limit" of 10GB and a "hard limit" of 15GB.

In any case it should therefore be clear that the exact approach is not uniquely defined, but must be commensurate with the type of users and on the 'actual use they make of the available storage space in the server shares.

Assigning the Grace Period

Before we named the *"grace period"* as the period of time which is allowed to exceed the limits imposed by the *"soft limit"*. The default value is seven days, as now we see how to change it at system-wide or for individual user/group. The command is always *edquota*, and to change it at the global level do:

```
sudo edquota -t
```

with the editor you'll see something like this:

```
Grace period before enforcing soft limits for users:
Time units may be: days, hours, minutes, or seconds
   Filesystem        Block grace period      Inode grace period
   /dev/sda1         7days                   7days
```

we see how we can define a different time for *inode* or *block*, using the keywords *days, hours, minutes or seconds*.

Instead, to assign the "grace period" to the specific user projects1, we will use the command:

```
sudo edquota -Tu projects1
```

or for group *projects* with the command:

```
sudo edquota -Tg projects
```

In both cases, the procedure is the same as that already seen.

Quote management

It is very important, even without a quota assignment, to learn how periodically check the disk space used.

repquota

we can do the manual control with the simple *repquota* command:

```
sudo repquota /
```

that will generate the complete list of users, current use of resources, and the quotas assigned. For example something like this:

```
*** Report for user quotas on device /dev/sda1
Block grace time: 7days; Inode grace time: 7days
                          Block limits              File limits
User            used    soft    hard   grace   used  soft  hard  grace
--------------------------------------------------------------------
root       -- 1737104      0       0           66129     0     0
sbsadmin   --      84      0       0              13     0     0
user1      --      20      0       0               5     0     0
projects1  +-  547560  500000  700000  5days    7224     0     0
projects2  --      20      0       0               5     0     0
```

The two characters "--" after the username is a quick way to see when you exceed the limits of space (the first character) or files (the second one). If these limits are exceeded, we see the "+" character. In this example we can immediately see that the user "projects1" has crossed the first threshold.

The column "grace" is normally empty, unless we passed one of the "soft limit". This example shows that the "grace" is still guaranteed for five days (*5days*), after that the word "none" appears to indicate that the grace period is over.

We get the same result for the group with the command:

```
sudo repquota -g /
```

The output will be almost the same as before, of course we see the list of groups instead of users.

In the preparation phase would be a good idea to turn on the quotas without assigning specific values. In this way we could understand how disk space is used by users. So, *repquota* is also a useful tool to estimate and then decide a fair and efficient policy with which to assign the "Disk Quotas."

warnquota

warnquota is a handy tool that helps us to keep the users exceeding the quota under control. It runs every day and sends an email notice to the user and the system administrator.

Setup is simple, and can be done easily by *debconf*, taking care to answer simple questions that are asked. Type:

```
sudo dpkg-reconfigure -plow quota
```

Debconf will change the configuration file:

```
/etc/warnquota.conf
```

create the script in *cron.daily*:

```
/etc/cron.daily/quota
```

and enable it, putting *run_warnquota="true"* in the file:

```
/etc/default/quota
```

If instead we prefer to change the values manually, we can do it easily with our favorite editor.

Insight

Now let's see a simple list of things that might be useful and which perhaps would be worth expanding on its own. The examples described here do not apply if we have installed a member server in Active Directory.

Print services

We haven't talked at all about Printer Sharing. Here we would open another front involving CUPS and the automatic distribution printer drivers to Windows clients. Samba supports this feature, and the best place to learn this technique are the official guides.

GUI admin clients

We have already seen how to manage the permissions from Windows on Samba share. There are also GUI that allows us to manage users and passwords in a simple way, especially when the options to set are a bit "exotic", like the password expiration or the list of workstations from which a user can logon. There are many, with web browser we can use *Samba Web Administration Tool (called SWAT)* or *LDAP admin account*. From Windows *LDAP Admin* or also the "User Manager for Domains", the official tool provided from Microsoft Windows NT (is not a joke) to administer the various aspects and flags.

Samba commands

Samba comes with a series of commands useful for the Administrator, like *pdbedit* to administer users and groups or the plethora of available *net commands*. For example, with the command:

```
sudo net rpc rights list -U Administrator
```

we get this:

```
       SeMachineAccountPrivilege  Add machines to domain
         SeTakeOwnershipPrivilege  Take ownership of files or other objects
              SeBackupPrivilege  Back up files and directories
             SeRestorePrivilege  Restore files and directories
       SeRemoteShutdownPrivilege  Force shutdown from a remote system
         SePrintOperatorPrivilege  Manage printers
            SeAddUsersPrivilege  Add users and groups to the domain
          SeDiskOperatorPrivilege  Manage disk shares
```

which are Administrator rights. With *"net rpc right"* commands we can assign administrative right to other users.

If we type

```
sudo pdbedit -L -v Jack
```

we get:

```
Unix username:         jack
NT username:           jack
Account Flags:         [UX      ]
User SID:              S-1-5-21-1491279793-2809991009-2777690449-11012
Primary Group SID:     S-1-5-21-1491279793-2809991009-2777690449-513
Full Name:             jack
Home Directory:
HomeDir Drive:         K:
Logon Script:          jack.bat
Profile Path:
Domain:                STENOIT
Account desc:
Workstations:
Munged dial:
Logon time:            0
Logoff time:           never
Kickoff time:          never
Password last set:     0
Password can change:   0
Password must change:  0
Last bad password   :  0
Bad password count  :  0
Logon hours         :  FFFFFFFFFFFFFFFFFFFFFFFFFFFFFFFFFFFFFFFFFFFF
```

which are all *jack* settings that can we change with *pdbedit* command.
I can also use *netusermod*, but certainly the standard samba command is more complete. Type *"man pdbedit"* to see all switches.

File lock

We are administering a server with shared files, and file locking is important. Typically we do not need to worry, Samba "standard" have resolved most issues, but in some cases (such as the "usual" Microsoft Access mdb file) we must do it by hand.

For example, we could hear of *"Opportunistic Locking"*, a technique invented by Microsoft to boost network performance, which in some cases with Samba does not produce the desired effects.

Again, needless to say, it's all written in the official guide.

Security

Now the communication between Samba and OpenLDAP is unsafe. In our case the problem is minimal because both services are on the same hardware. But if we have more than one LDAP server can not ignore this aspect.

Conclusions

We must be honest, *we thought it was easier.* I'm not ashamed to say that this is what I thought when I first came across these issues.

But if we learn to manage well Los (**L**inux**O**penldap**S**amba) Amigos (do not forget DNS/DHCP) tomorrow (almost) we can install a network with Windows, because you know the concepts (even more deeply than others), only having to find out *"how"* but not *"why"*.

In the meantime we have learned what is behind those clicks ...

9

Mail Server

We shouldn't be surprised if the e-mail has become the most used Internet service. Its popularity and versatility have made it an indispensable tool for anyone.

Initially, the e-mails were suitable only for short messages, but after the advent of MIME (*Multipurpose Internet Mail Extension* and other types of decoding schemes, like *UUencode)*, it has also made possible to send formatted documents, photographs, audio and video files.

In this chapter we will configure an official and modern Mail Server with indispensable spam and virus filters.

There are some requirements to be fulfilled to make our installation complete and operational:

- ✔ Our domain *stenoit.com* must be registered with an official Internet Service Provider.
- ✔ The eth0 interface connected to the Internet must have a fixed IP address and our Internet Provider must have a PTR record in its DNS pointing to *mail.stenoit.com*
- ✔ The *maintainer* of our domain, if also manages the public DNS of *stenoit.com* domain, must create an *Mail Exchanger Record* (MX record) for our public IP address. In this way, e-mail should be routed directly to our server.

If we do not have a fixed IP address, there is also a second chance: we can configure the server in relay mode.

In this modality, our server does not contact directly the recipients SMTP server, but forwards mail to our "official" server (which presumably are from our provider) that takes care of the rest. Internal mail messages to the company (e.g. *jack@stenoit.com* that writes to *lucy@stenoit.com*) will not leave outside but will be internally managed. The problem now is that we have to manually download the incoming mail from the provider's server and distribute it to our internal users. We'll see how to solve the problem with fetchmail.

A team effort

The complexity of this part is not the implementation of a basic SMTP/POP3 server (relatively trivial thing), but the configuration of the various passages that an e-mail must perform on a modern Mail Server system. Unfortunately we have to try to defend us against viruses and spam if we want to give a decent service and let our server survive for more than a couple of days before being banned from the others.

Our MTA (Postfix) is not able to do it alone, but it uses four other external software (Postgrey, Amavisd-new, Spamassassin, Clamav) to filter mail. Finally, a sixth (Dovecot) is responsible for delivering e-mail to the user.

The configuration proposed here is not the only possible, but is the result of a couple of years of *tuning* in a real installation that serves approximately two hundred users with several thousands of e-mails every day, excellent to get started!

This is the software that we use:

- ✔ *Postfix* : Our MTA (Mail Transfer Agent) that implements our SMTP server
- ✔ *Postgrey* : Service that implements *greylisting*
- ✔ *Clamav* : The anti-virus used by Amavisd-new to e-mail scan
- ✔ *Spamassassin* : Used by Amavisd-new to spam detect
- ✔ *Amavisd-new* : The content filter that analyzes e-mails with Clamav and Spamassassin
- ✔ *Dovecot* : IMAP and POP3 servers to allow our users to download mail from the server

Installation

We begin with the installation of services, then we're going to set up them one by one.

Postfix & Postgrey

We install them this way:

```
sudo apt-get install postfix postgrey
```

When *debconf* asks us, we select parameters:

```
-> Internet Site
-> mail.stenoit.com
```

Amavisd-new, Spamassassin and Clamav

These are the three filtering software, so we install them:

```
sudo apt-get install amavisd-new clamav clamav-daemon spamassassin
```

We install also some suggested packages, especially the compression and decompression utility used by *Amavisd-new* and *Clamav* to manage e-mail attachments.

```
sudo apt-get install ripole tnef arj bzip2 cabextract cpio file
gzip lha nomarch rar unrar-free unzip lzop rpm2cpio p7zip-full
pax zip zoo
```

Dovecot

And finally we install our POP and IMAP server that will deliver mail to our client

```
sudo apt-get install dovecot-pop3d dovecot-imapd
```

Which path does an e-mail follow?

Well, now the required software is installed. Let's see briefly, when the configuration is completed, what will happen when a new message arrives to our mail server:

1. *Postfix* checks sender and receiver with its security settings. If they did not pass, Postfix rejects the mail, otherwise forwards the message to Postgrey
2. *Postgrey* analyzes the sender and then responds to *Postfix* with a success or failure message. If the *Postgrey* answer is negative, *Postfix* rejects the e-mail, otherwise he forwards the message to *Amavisd-new*
3. *Amavisd-new* uses *Clamav* for virus checks. If *Clamav* finds a virus, *Amavisd-new* responds with fail to *Postfix* and the e-mail is rejected. Otherwise, *Amavisd-new* uses *Spamassassin* for subsequent spam control.
4. If *Spamassassin* thinks that e-mail is spam, *Amavisd-new* responds with fail to *Postfix* and the e-mail is rejected.
5. If *Amavisd-new,* after virus and spam controls, does a positive response, *Postfix* delivers the mail on the recipient's mailbox.

Our email is taking a long and complicated path! This has a cost in performance, but to try to avoid junk mail or virus infections, it is worth.

The used term "reject" is generic, in fact the e-mail can be also stored and reported, or delivered to the end user with a warning. It is up to us to decide the behavior that most satisfy us.

MTA

We start the configuration of our Mail Server. The first step is to provide a basic *Postfix* installation.

Postfix is a popular, scalable and secure MTA written by Witse Venema while working at IBM. Originally it was known as *Vmailer*, and was also marketed by IBM as *Secure Mailer*. In 1999, his name has become definitively Postfix.

Postfix is a reliable, fast, extremely powerful and versatile MTA, while maintaining a relatively simple configuration file to read and maintain.

Configuration

We start with the basic configuration that is achieved by modifying the file */etc/postfix/main.cf* :

```
sudo nano /etc/postfix/main.cf
```

debconf has already set the basic parameters correctly, but we check that this is true, and if some are missing we provide a fix.

myhostname e mydomain

We define the host name of our internet server, by default the first is the value returned by *gethostbyname()* function, the second is the domain name:

```
myhostname = sbs.stenoit.com
mydomain = stenoit.com
```

myorigin

This identifies the domain names from which we assume local mails arrive and from which they are sent. It's harder to explain than to write. Since we don't need multiple domains, we set this parameter equal to *mydomain*:

```
myorigin = $mydomain
```

mydestination

This parameter specifies which domains this machine will deliver locally, instead of forwarding to another machine. For these destinations, then, the e-mails are considered local and transferred to local mailboxes.

```
mydestination = $myhostname, localhost.$mydomain, localhost, $mydomain
```

mynetworks

This identifies networks (or the specific host), who send mail from this server. Default Postfix receives mail from all network interfaces installed, but allows you to send only from *loopback interface* (127.0.0.1) that, in our case of course, isn't good. The *mynetworks* parameter value can be a single host, an IP address and netmask to indicate a range of host or subnet, or any number of comma separated hosts or IP address associated with netmasks.

This parameter is very important, must be present and contain ONLY the networks or hosts allowed, otherwise your server becomes an open relay, i.e. a server through which anyone can send mail! The open relays are the preferred target by spammers, but are, fortunately, an almost extincted kind of MTA.

In our case the mail server will allow the 192.168.20 .* internal network to send mail through it:

```
mynetworks = 127.0.0.0/8, 192.168.20.0/24
```

masquerade_domains

Now our network users can send mail, but many software clients will use the *fully qualified domain name (FQDN)* of the host. To understand better: if our host is called *mybox* and my user is *myuser*, who receives the e-mails that we send, will see the sender in the form *myuser@mybox.stenoit.com* that isn't exactly what we want. Probably I haven't even a user on that host and the recipient user will fail to respond to our e-mails. We solve this problem with the *masquerade_domains* parameter. Postfix replaces the domain part with what is specified here.

```
masquerade_domains = $mydomain
```

Now all hosts on my network can successfully send mail through Postfix. For example, the sender of the e-mails will have for all an address like *steno@stenoit.com*.

alias_database and alias_maps

Generally they coincide and indicate the name of the file and how local aliases are organized. In essence it is a list of equivalences that allow you to assign multiple addresses to a single user:

```
alias_maps = hash:/etc/aliases
alias_database = $alias_maps
```

mailbox_size_limit

Maximum size of the mailbox. In this case we specify 0 (zero) which means no limit.

```
mailbox_size_limit = 0
```

home_mailbox

It specifies where the user's mail is saved in relation to its home. If we don't specify anything, mbox format is used and Postfix creates a file named *username* in */var/spool/mail*. But, instead, we will use the *Maildir* format, so that each received mail will create a separate file in */home/username/Maildir*

```
home_mailbox = Maildir/
```

More information can be found on the Postfix website.

SMTP Authentication

Now our MTA already works, but it is preferable to provide it with a minimum of security through the SMTP authentication and TLS encryption. If we have external users who must use the email, we must allow them to send it through with our server, as when they are physically in the company. With the current configuration, only e-mail addressed to the internal domain users are accepted, which is not optimal. With SMTP authentication we resolve this issue.

Configuration

Postfix

We need to configure Postfix to use SASL. To do this we modify the usual configuration file:

```
sudo nano /etc/postfix/main.cf
```

adding these parameters:

```
smtpd_sasl_auth_enable = yes
smtpd_sasl_type = dovecot
smtpd_sasl_path = private/auth-client
smtpd_sasl_local_domain = $mydomain
smtpd_sasl_security_options = noanonymous
broken_sasl_auth_clients = yes
relay_domains = *
```

We create the *smtpd_recipient_restrictions* section and add, among the other, the directive *permit_sasl_authenticated* so that Postfix allows authenticated users to overcome the restriction. These directives will be explained later in detail.

The section should become so:

```
smtpd_recipient_restrictions =
        permit_sasl_authenticated,
        permit_mynetworks,
```

```
reject_unauth_destination,
permit
```

TLS

We create now digital certificates that are required to use the *Transport Layer Security* (TLS) for securing user authentication.

Type these commands in sequence, responding to various questions. The essentials data are two:

1. Password used, obviously don't forget it.
2. The *Common Name* must be unique, for example first we give the name of the machine (SBS) and then, when it creates a *Certificate Authority* (cacert.pem), the domain name (stenoit).

```
openssl genrsa -des3 -rand /etc/hosts -out mta.key 1024
chmod 600 mta.key
openssl req -new -key mta.key -out mta.csr
sudo openssl x509 -req -days 3650 -in mta.csr -signkey mta.key -out mta.crt
openssl rsa -in mta.key -out mta.key.unencrypted
mv -f mta.key.unencrypted mta.key
openssl req -new -x509 -extensions v3_ca -keyout cakey.pem -out cacert.pem -days 3650
sudo mv mta.key /etc/ssl/private
sudo mv mta.crt /etc/ssl/certs/
sudo mv cakey.pem /etc/ssl/private/
sudo mv cacert.pem /etc/ssl/certs/
```

Now we configure Postfix to use TLS. This time we use the *postconf* command, so that if the parameter already exists, it is properly set.

```
sudo postconf -e 'smtpd_tls_loglevel = 1'
sudo postconf -e 'smtpd_tls_received_header = yes'
sudo postconf -e 'smtpd_tls_session_cache_timeout = 3600s'
sudo postconf -e 'tls_random_source = dev:/dev/urandom'
sudo postconf -e 'smtpd_tls_auth_only = no'
sudo postconf -e 'smtp_use_tls = yes'
sudo postconf -e 'smtpd_use_tls = yes'
sudo postconf -e 'smtp_tls_note_starttls_offer = yes'
sudo postconf -e 'smtpd_tls_key_file = /etc/ssl/private/mta.key'
sudo postconf -e 'smtpd_tls_cert_file = /etc/ssl/certs/mta.crt'
sudo postconf -e 'smtpd_tls_CAfile = /etc/ssl/certs/cacert.pem'
```

SASL

Simple Authentication and Security Layer (SASL) is an authentication framework often used, it also supports *Transport Layer Security* (TLS).

Postfix is already built to use SASL, and can be used to implement the *Cyrus SASL* and *Dovecot SASL*.

In our case we will use Dovecot, given that it has already been installed.

So we edit the configuration file Dovecot:

```
sudo nano /etc/dovecot/dovecot.conf
```

Let's go in the default *auth* and remove the comment from the *listen socket* option. Then set the following:

```
socket listen {
client {
      path = /var/spool/postfix/private/auth-client
      mode = 0660
      user = postfix
      group = postfix
  }
}
```

leaving the rest commented.

Finally restart Dovecot:

```
sudo /etc/init.d/dovecot restart
```

that's all.

Testing our MTA

Install the "telnet" package that is useful for tests, and refresh Postfix settings:

```
sudo apt-get install telnet
sudo postfix reload
```

From console connect with "telnet" on port 25 (the default for the SMTP server):

```
telnet localhost 25
```

We should get the response:

```
Trying 127.0.0.1...
Connected to localhost.
Escape character is '^]'.
220 sbs.stenoit.com ESMTP Postfix (Ubuntu)
```

Let's start the dialogue:

```
ehlo sbs.stenoit.com
```

Postfix responds:

```
250-sbs.stenoit.com
250-PIPELINING
250-SIZE 10240000
250-VRFY
250-ETRN
250-STARTTLS
250-AUTH PLAIN
250-AUTH=PLAIN
250-ENHANCEDSTATUSCODES
```

```
250-8BITMIME
250 DSN
```

We can see that STARTTLS is present.
We continue to write (press "enter" after every line):

```
mail from:test@gmail.com
rcpt to: sbsadmin@stenoit.com
data
subject: Test Mail
Hello, this is a email test
.
```

After the ".". Postfix should give a response similar to this:

```
250 2.0.0 Ok: queued as BFB8C20AB1
```

The code "BFB8C20AB1" is a random number that changes each time.
Now typing:

```
quit
```

We come out. If we have not received errors, the service works on a regular basis. We can maybe check if *sbsadmin* has really received an e-mail by looking at the file with our text editor. Simply go to */home/sbsadmin/Maildir/new* and we should see a text. For example:

```
sudo nano 1198938050.V803I22110bM48209.sbs
```

Aliases

We have configured Postfix to use */etc/postfix/aliases* for aliases, we make a small change to the file because we want that system e-mails are all addressed to our user *sbsadmin* rather than to root (which is probably disabled). But since *sbsadmin* is the user that we created at install time, Ubuntu should already have done the work for us. We check if it is true:

```
sudo nano /etc/aliases
```

At the beginning of the file we should see something like that (if there isn't, just add it):

```
root: sbsadmin
```

We exit from the editor and type:

```
sudo newaliases
```

Now the mail addressed to *root* will be forwarded to our user *sbsadmin*.

Dovecot

Dovecot is a *Mail Delivery Agent* designed to guarantee security. It supports most mailboxes types: we are interested in a particular way to *Maildir*, which is the format that we decided to use. This section explains how to configure it as *IMAP* and *POP3* server after having already used, as we have just seen, like a SASL framework for SMTP authentication.

Configuration

We open again in an editor the Dovecot configuration file:

```
sudo nano /etc/dovecot/dovecot.conf
```

As we have already noticed, the file is quite large, we change only what we need and leave the rest unchanged.

We enable POP3 and IMAP protocols and their "secure" counterparts:

```
protocols = pop3 pop3s imap imaps
```

we accept connections to all network interfaces:

```
listen = *
```

and we continue enabling *ssl* and plain text passwords:

```
disable_plaintext_auth = no
ssl = yes
ssl_cert_file = /etc/ssl/certs/mta.crt
ssl_key_file = /etc/ssl/private/mta.key
```

and set *Maildir* as mailbox format:

```
mail_location = maildir:~/Maildir
```

At the end we set the UIDL format (*Unique Mail Identifier*) to use, leaving the default that works properly with Microsoft Outlook:

```
pop3_uidl_format = %08Xu%08Xv
```

Authentication

In order to obtain our *"Single Signon"* we must ensure that Dovecot authenticates users using the same user and password used by Samba. In this way our users will always use the same account for both the file server and mail.

This can be done in different ways, here we will use PAM that uses LDAP for authentication. Let's open (if we have closed it) the */etc/dovecot/dovecot.conf* configuration file and add (or edit, better) the following parameter:

```
passdb pam {
  args = blocking=yes dovecot
}
```

In this way now Dovecot uses PAM with the "rules" configured in the file */etc/pam.d/dovecot*.

```
sudo nano /etc/pam.d/dovecot
```

It should already be properly set by Ubuntu, so:

```
#%PAM-1.0

@include common-auth
@include common-account
@include common-session
```

Now Dovecot, as we wanted, to authenticate a user will use PAM who first uses the local unix user and later will ask to LDAP server.

Spam

Now our server can send and receive mail from the whole world. That's all? Sadly not. It works, and in a perfect world populated by only honest people we could stop here.

What a pity it isn't like this, and we must defend ourselves from the ever growing number of people who populate the network and who want to sell us blue pills even at Christmas! We must at least try to make their life a little bit harder.

Unless we take appropriate measures, in short time an incredible amount of mail that we receive will be inevitably junk that we haven't requested. In a word: *Spam*. Some e-mail will also contain *viruses* and *malware*, and the sender could also be one of our unsuspecting friend. Spam and virus-infected mail are a true planetary misfortune. **A non-secure mail server has a short life**, soon we will be banned as "bad" by public lists and we are no longer able to send e-mail because rejected by other servers. In short, *a disaster.*

We have our own personal server for e-mail and we must, therefore, protect it. We will see here how to do it.

Fortunately the tools for controlling and limiting (not defeat definitively, note) this problem exist, we will configure everything said before: *Postfix* to a first level of mail check, *Postgrey* that implements the *graylisting, Amavisd-new* that explores our e-mails and calls other packages such as *Spamassassin* to protect your server from spam and *ClamAV* for virus scanning. Even our *Shorewall* will help finally with an important rule.

What we have to do is to let them to work together.

Small note: is it necessary to protect Linux from viruses? Yes, and the reason is simple: in our internal network most computers will have some version of Windows that is the preferred target of virus and malware. So prevention is always better than cure. Therefore let's try to avoid that junk arrives to our clients.

Let's start with Postfix.

Postfix

Our MTA is able to auto provide a first level of protection. We open our configuration file:

```
sudo nano /etc/postfix/main.cf
```

Postfix generally writes to the log the reason for rejection of an e-mail, and setting *smtpd_delay_reject* = *yes*, it shows the sender and *HELO* string that caused the rejection. Let's go to the bottom of the file and add:

```
smtpd_delay_reject = yes
```

We also reject all mail from servers that do not properly identify themselves using the HELO command (or EHLO) as required by the SMTP RFC standards. Add:

```
smtpd_helo_required = yes
```

Now we set a number of restrictions to be applied. Who does not pass these, is rejected even before entering.

Restriction in the HELO o EHLO commands

HELO and EHLO are used by the remote mail server to identify itself. The restrictions are applied in sequence one by one.

- ✔ *permit_mynetworks*: it accepts connections from any Mail Server listing in the *mynetworks* parameter in *main.cf* configuration file.
- ✔ *reject_invalid_hostname*: it refuses connections from all servers that do not identify themselves using a correct host name (*fully qualified hostname*)
- ✔ *permit*: it eventually accepts connections from servers that have passed the previous checks.

```
smtpd_helo_restrictions =
        permit_mynetworks,
        reject_invalid_hostname,
```

```
reject_non_fqdn_hostname,
permit
```

Restrictions on commands sent from remote servers

✔ *reject_unauth_pipelining* : enforces our server to reject connections from servers that send commands too fast. Many spammers do this to try to speed up the process of being sent junk mail.

✔ *permit* : as above, accepts connections from servers that have passed the previous checks.

```
smtpd_data_restrictions =
        reject_unauth_pipelining,
        permit
```

Restrictions on the mail senders that the server receives

To identify the senders the SMTP MAIL FROM command is used:

✔ *permit_mynetworks* : as above
✔ *reject_non_fqdn_sender* : rejects mail from all senders whose name is not specified in extended mode (always according to the *"fully qualified host name"*). Note that hosts of our network are likely to have a short host name, but in this case are already guaranteed by the previous rule.
✔ *reject_unknown_sender_domain* : rejects mail from unknown domains
✔ *permit* : as above

```
smtpd_sender_restrictions =
        permit_mynetworks,
        reject_non_fqdn_sender,
        reject_unknown_sender_domain,
        permit
```

Restrictions on the recipients of our mail that the server receives

Recipients are identified using the SMTP RCPT TO command:

✔ *permit_sasl_authenticated* : We've seen before with SMTP authentication. Allows access to who authenticates correctly.
✔ *reject_unverified_recipient* : always rejects mail towards an unknown user. However I noticed that if the receiving server implements Postgrey this parameter actually prevents us from sending him mail because of refusal to validate the user imposed by functioning Post-

grey itself. We pay attention to log, and optionally disable the restriction for that domain.

✔ *permit_mynetworks* : as above

✔ *reject_unknown_recipient_domain* : reject the mail when our mail server is not the final destination and the target is not a valid domain

✔ *reject_unauth_destination* : reject the mail when the target domain is not one of those served by our server (defined by the *mynetworks* parameter) or is not among the domains defined in *relayhost*. This prevents that our server is used as *open relays*

✔ *check_policy_service* : this let Postfix use an external service for additional controls. In our case **inet:127.0.0.1:10023** passes control to Postgrey to implement the *graylisting*. We will see later.

✔ *permit* : as above.

```
smtpd_recipient_restrictions =
        permit_sasl_authenticated,
        reject_unverified_recipient,
        permit_mynetworks,
        reject_unknown_recipient_domain,
        reject_unauth_destination,
        check_policy_service inet:127.0.0.1:10023,
        permit
```

Well, at this point Postfix will already reject autonomously a part of unsolicited mail. Another thing we could implement is a check if the sender appears in public lists of recognized spammers (*RBL lists*). However, the disadvantages are often more than the advantages: the system is slow and, worse still, often the lists are not accurate. With Postgrey as an ally, I prefer not to implement it.

Restriction tests

Postfix provides a large amount of parameters, it is sometimes useful to test a restriction before you throw away the mail. Here are some useful parameter to use during test or tuning phase.

soft_bounce

Add it with the *postconf* command (but of course we could also edit the file */etc/postfix/main.cf*, is the same thing) and we reload the Postfix configuration:

```
sudo postconf -e "soft_bounce = yes"
sudo postfix reload
```

When set to **yes**, the *hard reject responses* (5xx) are converted into *soft reject responses* (4xx). In this way the sender server, after a delay, operates a retry.

Setting this parameter allows us to check the log file and see what our server refuses. In this way we have time, if necessary, to adjust the configuration and wait for the new attempt.

Once you find the best configuration we can remove *soft_bounce* and reload Postfix configuration.

warn_if_reject

By placing this parameter to other directives, Postfix instead of refusing mail reports a **warning** in the log.

So, if we are not sure what effects can have a new restriction, this parameter allows us to check first and then eventually set the restriction as effective. For example:

```
smtpd_recipient_restrictions =
        reject_unverified_recipient,
        permit_mynetworks,
        warn_if_reject reject_invalid_hostname,
        reject_unknown_recipient_domain,
        reject_unauth_destination,
        check_policy_service inet:127.0.0.1:10023,
        permit
```

We can notice the *warn_if_reject* preceding the *reject_invalid_hostname* rule: so if a client uses an *invalid HELO hostname* when sending messages, it falls in our restriction, but with this set Postfix writes in the log a *warning* and accepts the mail.

Reload Postfix and check there are no errors:

```
sudo postfix reload
```

Very good. Now only *official servers* can send mail to us. But this is not enough, is just the first step.

Postgrey

Now proceed with the configuration of a service that alone, so simple and ingenious, will sweep away from our server most spam. Indispensable.

Previously we set the Postfix *check_policy_service* directive for use Postgrey as an external service of greylisting.

But, what is the *graylisting*?

You probably already know the *whitelists* (the good list) and *blacklists* (the bad list) concepts. Postgrey is implemented with an intermediate level between the two, called *greylisting*.

This system uses a very simple concept: given the high number of e-mails that spammers send, they rarely try more than once to send mail to a recipient.

With Postgrey our server takes advantage of this, rejecting temporarily all e-mails from unknown senders by reporting them that the recipient's mailbox is not available at this time, waiting the second attempt that a good server always does.

Simple, effective and ingenious, without Bayesian filters or other gadgets, I guarantee you, this system wipes out more than 95% of spam!

What does Postgrey make

With the default configuration, we now see, in short, what happens when Postgrey controls a new e-mail that comes from an unknown sender:

- ✔ Postgrey rejects mail. Postfix informs the sender server that the mailbox of user is currently not available
- ✔ Postgrey stores in the *greylist* the following set of values: source host's IP address, e-mail sender, e-mail of the recipient.
- ✔ With the next attempt made by the sending server, if it hasn't spent the time delay (300 seconds), Postgrey continues to reject the mail. This is to avoid the too fast resending sometimes operated by spammers.
- ✔ If the delay time has elapsed, Postgrey accepts the mail and stores the triplet (source host IP address, e-mail sender address, e-mail recipient address) in its *whitelist* for *"max age"* time (30 days)

As we see the "triplet" for default remains in the whitelist for 30 days, so who regularly sends e-mail to us is no longer being delayed by Postgrey but accepted immediately.

Side effects?

Well, it has some flaws, but they are certainly tolerable:

- ✔ Delay in delivery of messages, usually a few minutes, but on high traffic servers can also be a few hours.
- ✔ Delivery problems can occur when the sender's SMTP server is not a single server, but a pool of systems or an entire sub-network, like Hotmail for example. The message, in this case, can be refused multiple times because each time the "triplet" data may be different. In general, after all the triplets were obtained and after a number of attempts, the message is successfully delivered. To handle these cases you can still use the *Whitelist* feature.

We also point out that the system load increases a little, because each new message must be received twice, but the benefits we get are still *great*.

So let's enjoy *greylisting* until it works, I fear that if it is implemented on a large scale (but I think the big providers with high volume of traffic they will hardly) spammers will begin to propose effective countermeasures... an endless war.

Configuration

The basic configuration of Postgrey is very simple. In fact, practically we cannot do anything. In the Postfix *smtpd_recipient_restrictions* parameter we have already set:

```
check_policy_service inet:127.0.0.1:10023
```

That is enough for us. We can restart the service to ensure that work:

```
sudo /etc/init.d/postgrey restart
```

More Postgrey configurations can be made by editing the default service configuration file:

```
sudo nano /etc/default/postgrey
```

particularly interesting are the two parameters:

- ✔ *--delay* :   delay: defines how many seconds the message is put in greylisting. Default is 300 seconds.
- ✔ *--max-age* : defines how many days a sender that has previously passed the test, it remained in *whitelist* generated by Postgrey. As long as they are here, will be accepted without further verification. By default is 30 days.

To change these parameters we have to put them in POSTGREY_OPTS variable, and restart the service.

For example, to bring the *delay* to 180 seconds and the *max age* to 60 days:

```
POSTGREY_OPTS="--inet=127.0.0.1:10023 --delay=180 --max-age=60"
```

Postgrey stores its data in Berkeley DB format in the folder:

```
/var/spool/postgrey
```

We can customize the *Whitelist* by editing the file where it lists the domains that do not filter:

```
sudo nano /etc/postgrey/whitelist_clients
```

or the recipients do not filter:

```
sudo nano /etc/postgrey/whitelist_recipients
```

Content Filter with Amavisd-new

For this configuration we have chosen applications that are known for the smooth level of security that they offer and the ease with which their own configuration files can be changed. As we now understand, by default, our MTA will listen on port 25 for incoming mail. When new mail arrives, after its canonical restrictive controls (including Postgrey), the Postfix forwards it to *Amavisd-new* on port 10024. Amavisd-new then checks the message through various filters and returns it to Postfix on port 10025. Finally, the message is sent to the recipient's mailbox.

A Corporal with two Soldiers

What is Amavisd-new? "Corporal" *Amavisd-new* is a framework for filtering content using applications that support the recognition of viruses and spam. He will use two "soldiers" for its battle: *ClamAV* for virus filtering and *Spamassassin* for spam. Spamassassin, then can use other low-level applications, such as *Vipul's Razor* and *DCC* (this case is not covered in this book).

Compared to other spam control technologies such as *RBL* (*Real-time Blackhole List*, a term that is often incorrectly called *DNSBL* technology) or *DNS blacklist* (which is the website publication of a list of IP addresses that should be blocked because they are a source of spam), Spamassassin does not accept or reject an e-mail based on a single test. This software, however, performs a check list, also using external applications, to calculate a score for each e-mail. This score is determined by:

✔ Bayesian filter
✔ Static rules based on regular expressions
✔ Distributed and collaborative networks (RBL, Razor, Pyzor, DCC)

Based on the customizable score, the mail will be rejected or accepted.

When Amavisd-new receives the alert that the mail contains viruses or spam, it can do three different things:

✔ **'PASS'**: The recipient also receives the mail
✔ **'DISCARD'**: The recipient does not receive the mail and the sender does not receive any notification that mail delivering is failed. If we have enabled this feature, the message is quarantined.
✔ **'BOUNCE'**: The recipient does not receive the mail and the sender receives a failure notification. No notification, however, is sent if the mail contains a virus, and the sender is identified as "fake".

✔ **'REJECT'**: The recipient does not receive the e-mail and the sender receives a notification from Postfix that mail delivering is failed.

The main difference between BOUNCE and REJECT is about who prepares this *Delivery Status Notification* (DSN). With REJECT is our MTA (Postfix) that prepares and delivers, with BOUNCE is Amavisd-new that does it (generally this contains further details). Since Postfix does not support the functionality REJECT, therefore for us the valid parameters remain PASS, DISCARD and BOUNCE.

In Amavisd-new, these options are indicated by **D_PASS**, **D_DISCARD** and **D_BOUNCE** and are configured with the parameters:

✔ **$final_spam_destiny**
✔ **$final_virus_destiny**
✔ **$final_banned_destiny**
✔ **$final_bad_header_destiny**

In our configuration we will set Amavisd-new so that spam and viruses are trashed (D_DISCARD), and since we do not disable the quarantine, the junk mail will end up there. If we wanted to disable quarantine the mail would be lost.

Some other notes about quarantine. Amavisd-new can quarantine the e-mail when the mail is spam/virus, or it can send it to another e-mail address for it to be analyzed by a human operator to maybe look for false positives. So basically, for example, we direct all the spam to *spam@stenoit.com* and virus to *virus@stenoit.com*, or alternatively save it to a directory on our server. Amavisd-new allows us to specify the directory for the quarantine with the **$QUARANTINEDIR** parameter. However, you can choose different folders for spam and viruses.

Now we configure the system to use Amavisd-new, beginning with Postfix and Spamassassin, and then finishing with Clamav.

Postfix

Still Postfix. We need to change the file where its services are defined by adding one for Amavisd-new and configure it so that it is used.

Edit the **master.cf** file (be careful, not *main.cf*), where Postfix service settings are specified:

```
sudo nano /etc/postfix/master.cf
```

and add at the bottom:

```
## AMAVISD-NEW
##
amavis    unix    -    -    -    -    2    smtp
    -o smtp_data_done_timeout=1200
    -o smtp_send_xforward_command=yes
    -o disable_dns_lookups=yes


127.0.0.1:10025    inet    n    -    -    -    -    smtpd
    -o content_filter=
    -o smtpd_restriction_classes=
    -o smtpd_delay_reject=no
    -o smtpd_client_restrictions=permit_mynetworks,reject
    -o smtpd_helo_restrictions=
    -o smtpd_sender_restrictions=
    -o smtpd_recipient_restrictions=permit_mynetworks,reject
    -o smtpd_data_restrictions=reject_unauth_pipelining
    -o smtpd_end_of_data_restrictions=
    -o mynetworks=127.0.0.0/8
    -o smtpd_error_sleep_time=0
    -o smtpd_soft_error_limit=1001
    -o smtpd_hard_error_limit=1000
    -o smtpd_client_connection_count_limit=0
    -o smtpd_client_connection_rate_limit=0
    -o smtpd_milters=
    -o local_header_rewrite_clients=
    -o local_recipient_maps=
    -o relay_recipient_maps=
    -o receive_override_options=no_header_body_checks,no_unknown_recipient_checks
```

What have we done? With this change we have defined two new "services": a*mavis* for the delivery of mail via SMTP to the content filter, and the *reinjection port 10025* where we expect the answer.

We've not finished, we are looking for the line (above) where "pickup" is written and make it become like this:

```
pickup    fifo  n    -    n    60    1    pickup
    -o content_filter=
    -o receive_override_options=no_header_body_checks
```

This means that local messages (like those generated by the server itself with crond for postmaster or root or whomever) are not filtered.

Finally we make a last change to the *main.cf* file:

```
sudo nano /etc/postfix/main.cf
```

where we instruct Postfix to use the content filter through the service defined on port 10024. Then add at the bottom:

```
content_filter = amavis:[127.0.0.1]:10024
receive_override_options=no_address_mappings
```

This tells us that we could, by specifying a different IP address, also use an external server for content filter.

Now two settings here deserve an brief explanation. First the *receive_override_options* are set to *no_address_mappings*. This disables all address mappings. Our virtual aliases for example are not considered at first. Then the e-mail is sent to Amavisd-new and in the end it returned to the *127.0.0.1:10025* service that sets a lot of options. One of those options is the *receive_override_options* again. But this time the *no_address_mappings* setting is left out. So at this stage Postfix finally checks your virtual aliases. It has to be done like this or otherwise our aliases would be evaluated twice which leads to mails sent twice. The other options are used to disable checks that Postfix has already done during the first stage.

Amavisd-new

Now is the turn of Amavisd-new. For customizations Ubuntu gives us a special empty file, so that we do not risk to compromise the default configuration:

```
sudo nano /etc/amavis/conf.d/50-user
```

We set the variable **$mydomain** with our domain name:

```
$mydomain = 'stenoit.com';
```

and change the name of the host with the variable **$myhostname.**

```
$myhostname = 'sbs.stenoit.com';
```

find the following line and add our domain:

```
@local_domains_maps = ( [".$mydomain", ".stenoit.com"] );
```

We continue with Spamassassin part of Amavisd-new. This means that any message that is addressed to a recipient that is considered local (**@local_domains**) will have X-Spam-Status, X-Spam-Score and X-Spam-Level headers added. The value "undef" is programmed to mean "lower than any possible score".

```
$sa_tag_level_deflt = undef;
```

This is the spam point level of the mails. Any mail with a score higher than **$sa_tag2_level_deflt** will be considered spam. Amavisd-new will add a prefix "[SPAM]" to the subject which is then sent to the recipient.

```
$sa_tag2_level_deflt = 5.0;
```

This value defines the Score on which the mail should be quarantined by Amavisd-new. It also defines the level above which the sender is informed (Delivery Status Notification, DSN) that the message was not delivered. No DSN is sent, however, if the **$sa_dsn_cutoff_level** is set to a value less than the number of points (see below).

Since we absolutely don't want to alert spammers that we have blocked their mail, we set the parameter at the absurd value of 10000.

```
$sa_kill_level_deflt = 10000;
```

Until now, all spam is sent to our users by changing only the subject. However, when later we define the variable **$spam_quarantine_to**, in fact each of these e-mails will be quarantined and sent to those defined by the parameter, with modified subject and header.

This parameter defines the score beyond which we are not interested to send the notification (DSN) to the sender. We can leave this value since we are not interested to send any notification (we'll change D_BOUNCE in D_DISCARD below).

```
$sa_dsn_cutoff_level = 9;
```

Beyond this level, the mail is not even placed in quarantine:

```
$sa_quarantine_cutoff_level = 20;
```

As we have said many times, it is not our intention to send any notification to the senders. All mails end up in quarantine. However we prefer to send mail to the person responsible for monitoring the messages instead of a directory of quarantine: the filters are not perfect and there may be some false positives. To do this we define the recipients, and the quarantine directory will be disabled automatically:

```
$final_virus_destiny = D_DISCARD;
$final_spam_destiny = D_DISCARD;
$final_banned_destiny = D_DISCARD;
```

The following addresses will become, then, **virus@stenoit.com** and **spam@stenoit.com**.

```
$virus_quarantine_to = "virus\@$mydomain";
$banned_quarantine_to = "spam\@$mydomain";
$bad_header_quarantine_to = "spam\@$mydomain";
$spam_quarantine_to = "spam\@$mydomain";
```

Now we define the addresses to notify. These recipients will receive notifications about found virus, to disable the notification just comment the line.

```
$virus_admin = "postmaster\@$mydomain";
$banned_admin = "postmaster\@$mydomain";
```

Here we define who should be the sender of the notifications:

```
$mailfrom_notify_admin = "postmaster\@$mydomain";
$mailfrom_notify_recip = "postmaster\@$mydomain";
```

```
$mailfrom_notify_spamadmin = "postmaster\@$mydomain";
$hdrfrom_notify_sender = "amavisd-new <postmaster\@$mydomain>";
```

and, to recognize it easily, the string to be prefixed to the subject of the mail that we consider SPAM:

```
$sa_spam_subject_tag = '[SPAM] ';
```

Amavisd-new uncompresses e-mail attachments to check for viruses. Before we installed the necessary packages, but now we need to enable support for files compressed with LHA/LZH that are disabled by default:

```
$lha = "lha";
```

Let's change the database aliases to avoid adding specified e-mail recipients. We have chosen to send all notifications to the administrator.

```
sudo nano /etc/aliases
```

Enter "virus" and "spam". The file should look like this:

```
root:           sbsadmin
virus:          root
spam:           root
postmaster:     root
clamav:         root
```

All notifications will be delivered to user *sbsadmin*. Let us not forget that after editing the file I have to always run:

```
sudo newaliases
```

to ensure that the changes become effective.

The last thing we need to do is to configure Amavisd-new to use Spamassassin and Clamav as antispam and antivirus filters.
We edit the file:

```
sudo nano /etc/amavis/conf.d/15-content_filter_mode
```

and remove the command from the rows that are affected. In this way:

```
#
# Default antivirus checking mode
# Uncomment the two lines below to enable it back
#

@bypass_virus_checks_maps = (
   \%bypass_virus_checks, \@bypass_virus_checks_acl, \$bypass_virus_checks_re);

#
# Default SPAM checking mode
# Uncomment the two lines below to enable it back
#

@bypass_spam_checks_maps = (
   \%bypass_spam_checks, \@bypass_spam_checks_acl, \$bypass_spam_checks_re);
```

```
#
```

We've finished. I grant that it can be really difficult to get out from the many options, but the important thing is that the end result is what we want, and there's no doubt about this.

Spamassassin

We just have to enable the Spamassassin. Simply edit the file:

```
sudo nano /etc/default/spamassassin
```

and set the parameter:

```
ENABLED=1
```

Clamav & Freshclam

Amavisd-new can use a wide range of antivirus that includes all the most popular players. We decided to use **clamav** since it is open source and freely available.

If instead we want to use a different one, let's look at the file:

```
/etc/amavis/conf.d/15-av_scanners
```

Which contains a section for each supported antivirus. Just uncomment the operative one, to have it enabled (we can also leave more than one).

Configuration

Clamav does not require a particular configuration, we only need to integrate it with Amavisd-new.

The only thing to do is allow users that start services to interact each other. Then assign the user "clamav" to the group "amavis" and the user "amavis" to the group "clamav"

```
sudo adduser amavis clamav
sudo adduser clamav amavis
```

We try to update the virus definitions:

```
sudo freshclam
```

We should get something like this:

```
ClamAV update process started at Fri Aug 27 15:00:40 2010
main.cvd is up to date (version: 52, sigs: 704727, f-level: 44, builder: sven)
daily.cld is up to date (version: 11719, sigs: 116535, f-level: 53, builder: arnaud)
bytecode.cvd is up to date (version: 39, sigs: 9, f-level: 53, builder: edwin)
```

Start of services

To make sure that all configurations are active we must now restart all services. Clamav has two daemons, one for scanning (*clamav-daemon*) and one to update the database of known viruses (*clamav-freshclam*), but they are run in pairs.

Type:

```
sudo /etc/init.d/clamav-freshclam restart
sudo /etc/init.d/clamav-daemon restart
sudo /etc/init.d/dovecot restart
sudo /etc/init.d/postfix restart
sudo /etc/init.d/postgrey restart
sudo /etc/init.d/spamassassin restart
sudo /etc/init.d/amavis restart
```

Wow. Our Mail Server with antispam and antivirus filters is ready! Let's take a quick look at the log with the command:

```
tail -f /var/log/mail.log
```

that should show something like this:

```
Aug 27 15:17:32 amavis[31888]: Found decoder for    .zoo  at /usr/bin/zoo
Aug 27 15:17:32 amavis[31888]: Found decoder for    .lha  at /usr/bin/lha
Aug 27 15:17:32 amavis[31888]: Found decoder for    .doc  at /usr/bin/ripole
Aug 27 15:17:32 amavis[31888]: Found decoder for    .cab  at /usr/bin/cabextract
Aug 27 15:17:32 amavis[31888]: No decoder for       .tnef
Aug 27 15:17:32 amavis[31888]: Internal decoder for .tnef
Aug 27 15:17:32 amavis[31888]: Found decoder for    .exe  at /usr/bin/lha;/usr/bin/arj
Aug 27 15:17:32 amavis[31888]: Using primary internal av scanner code for ClamAV-clamd
Aug 27 15:17:32 amavis[31888]: Found secondary av scanner ClamAV-clamscan at
/usr/bin/clamscan
Aug 27 15:17:32 amavis[31888]: Creating db in /var/lib/amavis/db/; BerkeleyDB 0.39,
libdb 4.8
```

Amavisd-new have found the decoders for compressed files and *ClamAV* for virus scanning of attachments.

Filter Test

We can test the antivirus downloading *Eicar*, a fake virus to test it on purpose. Let's go to our home and type:

```
wget http://www.eicar.org/download/eicar.com
```

then let us listen to the log file:

```
sudo tail -f /var/log/mail.log
```

Now from internal network clients try to send an e-mail with this attached file to a user of our domain (eg *user1@stenoit.com*), we should see something like this:

```
Blocked INFECTED (Eicar-Test-Signature)
```

indicating that our virus was successfully detected.

Alternatively we can run the test from the console, but before doing so we must temporarily disable, comment out with "#" options "*pickup*" that we included in the file */etc/postfix/master.cf*. Postfix, otherwise, does not filter messages sent locally from the server. Always remember to give:

```
sudo postfix reload
```

after every change.

Now send a test mail from the console:

```
sendmail -f test@gmail.com user1@stenoit.com < eicar.com
```

In the log we see that the message is identified and blocked, and looking the e-mail at user 's *sbsadmin@stenoit.com* (in */home/sbsadmin/Maildir/cur*, remember that *virus@stenoit.com* is just an alias) will find the mail with the virus alert.

Firewall

We must allow traffic on ports used by Dovecot and also, for security purpose, force our network users to **always use our server to send mail**.

Edit the file :

```
sudo nano /etc/shorewall/rules
```

and add new rules (unless we have already enabled all the internal traffic in the default policy of Shorewall)

```
POP3/ACCEPT          loc      $FW
IMAP/ACCEPT          loc      $FW
POP3S/ACCEPT         loc      $FW
IMAPS/ACCEPT         loc      $FW
```

If we want to get mail even when we are outside the company, we must also allow external access:

```
POP3/ACCEPT          net      $FW
IMAP/ACCEPT          net      $FW
POP3S/ACCEPT         net      $FW
IMAPS/ACCEPT         net      $FW
```

The most important rule

Now we are filtering all incoming e-mails to protect our users from spam and viruses. But this is not enough, we must also avoid being banned from other mail servers. To do this we can not limit ourselves only to reject junk mail, we must also avoid sending them.

If users of our network use our server to send e-mails, Amavisd-new does already his job, but what happens if one of our user (or a guest) has its own e-mail account at GMail or Yahoo or any another, and uses the SMTP of these providers to deliver mail? If accidentally the laptop is infected and turned into a zombie at the mercy of spammers, we have a big problem: the infected computer could start to send a huge amount of SPAM through your provider and the sender unfortunately will see our innocent server and its IP address. Result? We'll be "banned", and in a very short time our server will no longer be able to send a single e-mail.

How to prevent this disaster? Simple, just put this rule in */etc/shorewall/rules*:

```
REDIRECT loc  smtp  tcp  smtp - !212.239.29.208,192.168.20.1
```

Where "212.239.29.208", remember, is the public IP address of our server. In this way, anyone who tries to pass through the firewall (with the exception of those who correctly point) using SMTP, is redirected locally on the server so that it will have the ability to filter and block junk mail from any of our local network.

To activate the rule, just restart the service

```
sudo shorewall restart
```

Relay

Let's step back a little. At the beginning of this chapter we mentioned the possibility of using a local mail server without having a public static IP address, and without having the possibility to modify the table of our public DNS domain.

The solution to this problem is relatively simple but, unfortunately, is more complex to manage because we need to have an external mail server for sending mail to users that are not part of our network. In addition we need to duplicate the local users on the external mail server.

But then, what advantage may have a configuration like this? Essentially two: first, we can use our spam and virus filters that we have set so far and that undoubtedly make safer our mailboxes, and secondly, the exchange of mail and attachments between members in our network are much faster because remain local without passing through remote mail servers on the Internet.

We proceed on the assumption that the external server is called *mailext.stenoit.com* and has IP address 212.239.29.208.

DNS

First, if the name of external and public domain is the same as internal (as in this particular case, *stenoit.com*) we must set our DNS correctly. See Chapter 5 on how to create a record that correctly resolves the host name we have chosen:

```
mailext.stenoit.com   212.239.29.208
```

Postfix

Since most of the mail server does not accept mail from IP addresses that are not recognized, for sending the mail we have to configure Postfix to forward all outgoing mail to public and authoritative relay *mailext.stenoit.com* who will then send e-mail to recipients. To be able to send e-mail with this external server we need to authenticate us. Before beginning we must so create at least one valid *username* with *password* on *mailext.stenoit.com*. And now, these are the basic steps to set up Postfix to use *SMTP Authentication* to send mail through our relay host with these user credentials.

Create a password maps file as follows:

```
sudo nano /etc/postfix/sasl_password
```

and insert this:

```
mailext.stenoit.com username:password
```

protect files:

```
sudo chown root:root /etc/postfix/sasl_passwd
sudo chmod 600 /etc/postfix/sasl_passwd
```

convert file on Postfix lockup table format:

```
sudo postmap /etc/postfix/sasl_passwd
```

edit the Postfix configuration file:

```
sudo nano /etc/postfix/main.cf
```

and set the parameters:

```
relayhost = mailext.stenoit.com
smtp_sasl_auth_enable = yes
smtp_sasl_password_maps = hash:/etc/postfix/sasl_passwd
smtp_sasl_security_options = noanonymous
```

now, after typing:

```
sudo postfix reload
```

all mail with domain not included in the Postfix parameter *mydestination* will be forwarded to *mailext.stenoit.com* that will send it to proper destination.

Fetchmail

The problem of outgoing mail is resolved quickly, but can we do the same for incoming e-mail? For internal e-mails there is no problem, but those from external domains will not come directly to our internal server, but will stop on *mailext.stenoit.com* where, of course, we have previously created all the appropriate mailboxes.

To resolve this issue we will use *Fetchmail*, a software that allows us to download e-mails from POP3 and IMAP server and then pass them to local users.

Installation and configuration

To install just type the simple command:

```
sudo apt-get install fetchmail
```

the first thing we must do is set it as a daemon, in this way every N minutes (that we define later) is going to pick up mail from *mailext*.

```
sudo nano /etc/default/fetchmail
```

and set the parameter:

```
START_DAEMON=yes
```

The *fetchmail* configuration comes with the following file:

```
sudo nano /etc/fetchmailrc
```

where we first enter the parameters:

```
# Download every 5 minutes
set daemon 300
# log with syslog
set syslog
```

The first parameter is the most important because it instructs fetchmail to download, if exists, e-mails every 5 minutes (300 seconds).

Then we can start to set the individual mailboxes to be downloaded using this syntax if, for instance, the users affected are *projects1* and *sales1*:

```
poll mailext.stenoit.com timeout 60 uidl proto POP3
  user "projects1" pass "mypwd" is projects1 here fetchall
  user "sales1" pass "mypwd" is sales1 here fetchall
```

So in our case at intervals of 5 minutes a *poll* on the external server is executed and all e-mails are downloaded and deleted (*fetchall*) through *POP3* on *mailext.stenoit.com* relating to specified users.

This is just a common example of how fetchmail is used. However, it has many parameters, see online help to solve special cases, or type:

```
fetchmail --help
```

to see a brief explanation.

Roundcube Webmail

We have LAMP up and running, why do not give users a convenient Webmail to read your mail with a browser? It could be very useful when you are away from home and you do not have their own computer.

There are many packages that perform this function, we will install *Roundcube Webmail*, a multilingual IMAP client created following Web 2.0 standards with a good user interface compatible with most browsers. With Roundcube you can have all the functionality of any e-mail client, including MIME support, address book, folder management, search and spell check messages. The package is written in PHP and, interestingly, it uses a database (in our case MySQL) to store data.

Acting on the "skin", the user interface is customizable in appearance, so the most willing will realize a "theme" that reflects the company's graphic layout.

Installation and configuration

Once again this procedure with Ubuntu is incredibly simple:

```
sudo apt-get install roundcube tinymce php-mdb2-driver-mysql
```

tinymce editor (optional) is written on *javascript* that will allow us to write the text of the e-mail in WYSIWYG mode.

During installation, debconf will make us some questions for Roundcube configuration and after that it will create the tables on the database. We respond in this way (remember that "admin" is password for MySQL "root" user, as defined during the installation of MySQL in Chapter 7):

```
Configure roundcube with dbconfig-common? ? => <Yes>
roundcube database type to use => mysql
Password for database administrator => admin
Roundcube MySQL application password => roundadmin
Confirm password => roundadmin
```

Now we activate *Roundcube* editing the file:

```
sudo nano /etc/roundcube/apache.conf
```

and uncomment the line:

```
Alias /roundcube /var/lib/roundcube
```

We configure two parameters by editing the file:

```
sudo nano /etc/roundcube/main.inc.php
```

setting the following values:

```
$rcmail_config['default_host'] = 'localhost';
$rcmail_config['mail_domain'] = 'stenoit.com';
```

on this way during login only the username and password are required (Round-cube could also be used to connect to other domains).

Do not forget the firewall if we want to access the webmail from outside, by adding the following rule in */etc/shorewall/rules*:

```
HTTP/ACCEPT              net     $FW
```

to allow access to the firewall via a browser.

Restart the services:

```
sudo /etc/init.d/apache2 restart
sudo shorewall restart
```

Now to access to Webmail Roundcube just point our favorite browser at:

```
http://sbs.stenoit.com/roundcube
```

Conclusions

This part has been a bit complicated, but I assure you that the result is excellent. Of course, it would be desirable to simplify it a little bit maybe combining some features (especially the content filter) directly on Postfix since by now virtually all mail servers filter messages.

Goodness knows! Maybe one day someone will think about it, in the meantime we don't have many alternatives to what we saw.

10

Proxy Server

With the NAT configuration seen in Chapter 6, we allowed all our clients network to browse internet. Each of them will be "masked" to the external network, our firewall will act as an intermediary in a transparent manner whatever the nature of our request is.

However, often this anarchy is not tolerated, the desire to control where, who and when our users request web pages or other services is very common.

To meet these needs, on this chapter we install and configure a Proxy Cache service. Later we'll see also how to use Shorewall to operate a control over Internet traffic.

The Proxy is software that is responsible to load internet web pages requests from our users, and to copy them locally on a transparent manner. In addition it can also operate the filter to grant users access to them.

But let's see on detail the main benefits of using a service like this:

- ✔ Users do not have direct access to the Internet but first query the cache server. In this way if a page has already been requested from another user, it is already present on local cache increasing significantly the speed of navigation.
- ✔ We can limit web browsing, for example, configuring the server so that users can not access certain websites or that browsing both completely free on predetermined time slots, for example, only during the lunch break.
- ✔ We can limit which users have access to the Internet.
- ✔ Security. The proxy is a filter between us and the Internet. By limiting users' freedom of the internal, risks are reduced.

We do not analyze all these aspects, we will implement one that is very common, which is to restrict web browsing to users that are members of a specific group created for the occasion on our Domain Controller Samba. To implement authentication will activate a special helper, and we need a File Server with LDAP as seen in Chapter 8.

To configure the client side, however, we will use WPAD (*Web Proxy Autodiscovery Protocol*), so users' browsers will automatically find the proxy server without manual intervention. WPAD need the web server installed in Chapter 7.

Squid

Proxy Cache, on a Linux environment, is almost synonym of "*Squid*". *Squid*, in fact, is a powerful software that provides proxy and cache for HTTP (*Hyper Text Transport Protocol*), FTP (*File Transfer Protocol*) and many other network protocols. It also supports SSL (*Secure Sockets Layer*), searches for caching DNS (*Domain Name Server*) and *transparent caching*, a name, this last one, that is a technique whereby each HTTP, FTP or otherwise in transit through the firewall is automatically redirected to proxy without any intervention on the clients. However this has particular limits that we will see later.

A server with Squid is therefore one valid solution for caching/proxy needs, being able to scale from small office to large enterprise, providing also tools for control and monitoring of critical parameters very accurately.

But be careful: *Squid is very hungry for memory*, more memory is available and more its performance increases. For small installations like ours there is no problem but, if the number of clients on the network would greatly increase, it can become a bottleneck.

Cases

First, let's see what we aim to do, the possibilities are many and various, we show two cases that are simple but complete, with user authentication. In both cases we allow web browsing only to users who are members of a specific group of samba domain named "*Internet*". In this way to enable or not "*user1*" to internet browsing, we will simply make it or not a member of the group.

Why two different settings? Because the one I think is the most interesting and complete requires that the Proxy resides on a different machine from where we installed the Domain Controller, otherwise it won't authenticate users. Squid is not a problem, and even the Samba, but using *Winbind* for authentication, which for its nature can not enumerate local users and groups, but only users of external "trusted" domains. It may seem strange but it isn't: Winbind is used on various contexts, for example, in case you want to authenticate Linux users on an external Microsoft Domain Controller.

However, if one day the number of users were to increase, would be a good idea to split the workload across multiple servers. In this case we could use this solution.

LDAP authentication (ldap_auth)

Squid supports authentication with several external helpers, simple passwd, LDAP, Samba and Microsoft Active Directory.

With this helper active the user must enter username and password that will be showed in the window from their browser. If authentication is successful, Squid will check that the user is also a member of the "Internet", in this case it allows navigation.

Installation

The installation is not difficult, so we install version 3 of the Squid Proxy Cache:

```
sudo apt-get install squid3
```

Configuration

The Squid configuration file is generous in the comments and the possible parameters are a lot. We save original configuration and start from a clean file by including only what we need.

```
sudo mv /etc/squid3/squid.conf /etc/squid3/squid.conf.orig
sudo nano /etc/squid3/squid.conf
```

Here's what to insert in the file:

```
visible_hostname sbs
http_port 3128
hierarchy_stoplist cgi-bin ?
acl apache rep_header Server ^Apache

cache_mem 8 MB
access_log /var/log/squid3/access.log squid
auth_param basic program /usr/lib/squid3/squid_ldap_auth \
                -b "ou=Users,dc=stenoit,dc=com" \
                -v3 -f "uid=%s" -h localhost
auth_param basic children 5
auth_param basic credentialsttl 30 minutes

authenticate_ip_ttl 9 hour

external_acl_type ldap_group ttl=5 children=5 \
                %LOGIN /usr/lib/squid3/squid_ldap_group \
                -b "ou=Groups,dc=stenoit,dc=com" \
                -B "ou=Users,dc=stenoit,dc=com" \
                -f "(&(memberUid=%v)(cn=%a))" -h localhost
```

```
acl internetfull external ldap_group internet

acl goodurl url_regex -i "/etc/squid3/goodurl"
acl badurl url_regex -i "/etc/squid3/badurl"
acl time_acl time M T W H F 8:30-19:00
refresh_pattern ^ftp: 1440 20% 10080
refresh_pattern ^gopher: 1440 0% 1440
refresh_pattern . 0 20% 4320
acl manager proto cache_object
acl localhost src 127.0.0.1/255.255.255.255
acl to_localhost dst 127.0.0.0/8

acl SSL_ports port 443
acl Safe_ports port 80 # http
acl Safe_ports port 21 # ftp
acl Safe_ports port 443 # https
acl Safe_ports port 70 # gopher
acl Safe_ports port 210 # wais
acl Safe_ports port 1025-65535 # unregistered ports
acl Safe_ports port 280 # http-mgmt
acl Safe_ports port 488 # gss-http
acl Safe_ports port 591 # filemaker
acl Safe_ports port 777 # multiling http
acl officialweb dst www.stenoit.com

acl CONNECT method CONNECT
acl password proxy_auth REQUIRED

http_access allow officialweb
http_access allow goodurl
http_access deny badurl
http_access allow manager localhost
http_access deny manager
http_access deny !Safe_ports
http_access deny CONNECT !SSL_ports
http_access allow password internetfull
http_access deny all

coredump_dir /var/spool/squid3
```

We give one brief explanation of the most significant parameters.

visible_hostname

The name of the proxy. Instead of "sbs" we could put "proxy" adding the reference to the file */etc/dnshosts* as seen in Chapter 5, so we can move the server easily by changing only the references in the DNS table.

http_port

The port on which the proxy is listening. 3128 is the default.

cache_mem

The memory used by Squid to speed up browsing. 8MB is the default, we can also go up, depending on how much RAM we have.

auth_param

One great feature of Squid is to allow access to the service only after authentication. Among the various authentication modes supported, there is one that uses the data stored on an LDAP server.

To use this feature we must first configure Squid, enabling user authentication, to use the **basic** scheme (other schemes are **NTLM** and **digest**, see the online guide for more info) that uses plain text users and passwords. The base directive that allows you to set user authentication is precisely *auth_param*, which takes as first argument the format to be used (in our case, *basic*), the second the directive (*program*) as the third argument and the parameter to configure.

The directive must be repeated for each parameter you want to configure, but the main program, which lets you specify the program to use to authenticate users using LDAP, is *squid_ldap_auth*:

```
auth_param basic program /usr/lib/squid3/squid_ldap_auth
                  -b "ou=Users,dc=stenoit,dc=com"
                  -v3 -f "uid=%s" -h localhost
```

-b indicates the base of the tree on which we perform the search, *-v3* indicates that the use of LDAP version 3, *-f* specifies the filter to search for user (*%s* indicates the user) and *-h* the LDAP server. Please note that the command should be entirely on a single line.

The following parameters:

```
auth_param basic children 5
auth_param basic credentialsttl 30 minutes
```

configure the helper so that there are five children processes (*children 5*) to accelerate the response, and that authentication is not requested again for thirty minutes (*credentialsttl 30 minutes*).

Then specifying:

```
acl password proxy_auth REQUIRED
http_access allow password
```

allow any user to successfully log in to browse the internet.

external_acl_type

Squid also allows a much more detailed control, allowing us to set different ACL depending on the user, maintained on LDAP, group membership. To obtain this result we must use its own special feature: the ability to extend ACLs using an external application, similar to what happens to authentication.

Squid ACLs include a special class, called *external,* which allows us to carry out a program by invoking the appropriate help through the *external_acl_type* directive. This takes as its argument a name that identifies the particular type of ACL, followed by the information necessary to call the external program.

To use as ACL the user membership (or not) to a specific group on LDAP, we use a special program, *squid_ldap_group,* distributed by Ubuntu with Squid, which allows us to verify this.

Here's the relevant extract:

```
external_acl_type ldap_group ttl=5 children=5
                  %LOGIN /usr/lib/squid3/squid_ldap_group
                  -b "ou=Groups,dc=stenoit,dc=com"
                  -B "ou=Users,dc=stenoit,dc=com"
                  -f "(&(memberUid=%v)(cn=%a))" -h localhost
```

(I remember once again that what is written must be entirely on a single line) and its ACL:

```
acl internetfull external ldap_group internet
```

In practice here we define an external *ldap_group* ACL, which uses that program, and then use it to create the new ACL to be used to impose different restrictions depending on group membership (in this case "*internet*").

The parameters *-b* and *-B* specify the section of the tree where users and groups reside, respectively, *%LOGIN* contains the authenticated user name, *-f* is the filter to verify that the user is member to the group.

The program *squid_ldap_group* takes as input a line containing user and group and returns the result (as required for use by *external_acl_type*) to standard output, so it can also be used from the command line for test purpose.

For example, this command verify that the user *"projects1"* is member of the group *"projects"* (note again and again: *the command must be on a single line!*):

```
echo "projects1 projects" | /usr/lib/squid3/squid_ldap_group -b
"ou=Groups,dc=stenoit,dc=com" -B "ou=Users,dc=stenoit,dc=com"  -f
"(&(memberUid=%v)(cn=%a))" -h localhost
```

The answer should be a simple *"OK"* if it is true, or an *"ERR"* if not.

The filter *-f* supports a special syntax in which we can use the variables *%v* and *%a* to indicate respectively the user name and the group name. If we find a matching entry, the program will be successful.

acl & http_access

The ACL commands (*Access Control List*) are used, as we have partially already seen, to define the types of controls to accept or not the request of users. For example with:

```
acl goodurl url_regex -i "/etc/squid3/goodurl"
```

we define an acl *"goodurl"* of type *"url_regex"* indicating as a parameter to an external file (option -*i*). This external file can list, for example, the Web sites to which we allow access to everyone. The behavior of the ACL, however, is defined below like enabling *goodurl* also for unauthenticated users by *http_access allow*.

We can understand better with another example:

```
acl mynet src 192.168.20.0/255.255.255.0
acl time_acl time M T W H F 12:00-13:30
```

These ACLs define a range of addresses that corresponds to my internal network, and a period of time, Monday to Friday from 12:00 to 13:30. And now look how to enable browsing during lunch to the sites specified in the file goodurl:

```
http_access allow mynet time_acl goodurl
```

We can also define the denial with an exclamation mark (*!*), for example to enable navigation in the period of time except in the sites defined in a new ACL named *"badurl"* we must add:

```
acl badurl url_regex -i "/etc/squid3/acl/badurl"
acl localnet src 192.168.20.0/255.255.255.0
acl time_acl time M T W H F 12:00-13:30
http_access allow mynet time_acl !badurl
```

It is important to know that the *http_access* directives **are evaluated in the insert order,** and that the evaluation stops on first match.

So such a directive:

```
http_access deny all
```

should be written at the end, otherwise none will ever be able to access to the internet.

In this regard, we return to examine our configuration file and look at the first three directives:

```
http_access allow localnet
http_access allow officialweb
http_access allow password internetfull
```

if a user accesses a web server in the intranet (*allow localnet*) or external to our company web site (*allow officialweb*) is allowed immediately, without evaluating user, password and "internet" group membership.

The other parameters are similar in concept, to a deeper insight we can read the original file *squid.conf.orig*, or the online documentation.

After each modification to the *squid.conf* file do not need to restart the service (which takes away a bit of time), but we just have to reload Squid settings in this manner:

```
sudo squid3 -k reconfigure
```

NTLM authentication (ntlm_auth)

We see now a very interesting alternative to what we saw before. This type of authentication is very similar to the previous one, but with the important difference that uses the **Microsoft Domain passthrough authentication**: the user's browser (either IE or Firefox or also Chrome from version 6) will automatically use the username and password used to logon to the Samba Domain, without requiring again as it does with *ldap_auth yet*.

Even with this method we can create a Samba group "Internet" whose members will be able to navigate *seamlessly*.

Let's see what happens, in fact,to hypothetical user "user1"

1. The user "user1" exists on the domain and is member of the "Internet" group. "user1" has access to the internet with its browser through the proxy transparently.
2. The user "user1" exists on the domain but is not member of the "Internet" group. "user1" receives an error message in the browser and does not have access to the Internet.
3. The user "user1" **does not exist on the domain**. The browser displays a dialog window asking for username and password. If we used a valid user and password of a user member of the "Internet" group, navigation is allowed.

Therefore, to enable a user of our network to the internet browsing will be very simple: just make it a member of the group established. The point three is very important: if we receive "guests" in our network, to enable them to browse just give them a user name and password created for the occasion. Then, even if this were to get back to other users of our domain, as explained in the point 2, they would not be able to use it.

Unfortunately, as mentioned above, its functioning requires us to have separate machines on which to run the proxy and the domain controller. In our case, therefore, we cannot use it.

But if we had a different configuration? If the Domain Controller was a different machine? If it was even a Microsoft Active Directory server?
So in both cases we can use this "helper". Now we will analyze both cases.

Samba installation

In both cases we suppose that we have a Proxy Server called *"sbsproxy"* on which we installed Squid3. We need to install *samba* and *winbind*:

```
sudo apt-get install samba winbind
```

Winbind does not need any configuration.

Samba Domain Controller

The configuration, however, is a little different.

Samba configuration

We configure Samba, and we *join the domain*. Here is the configuration file, we need just the *[global]* section.

```
sudo nano /etc/samba/smb.conf
```

In this way:

```
[global]
        unix charset = LOCALE
        workgroup = STENOIT
        netbios name = SBSPROXY
        server string = %h Member (%v)
        interfaces = eth1, lo
        bind interfaces only = Yes
        enable privileges = yes
        guest account = guest
        wins support = No
        security = domain
        ldap suffix = dc=stenoit,dc=com
        ldap user suffix = ou=Users
        ldap machine suffix = ou=Computers
        ldap group suffix = ou=Groups
        ldap idmap suffix = ou=Idmap
        ldap admin dn = cn=admin,dc=stenoit,dc=com
        idmap backend = ldap:ldap://sbs.stenoit.com
        idmap uid = 10000-20000
        idmap gid = 10000-20000
        winbind use default domain = yes
        ldap ssl = no
```

It's very similar to what we saw for the Domain Controller, but with important differences, first of all the *"security"* parameter which in this case indicates a *"member"* machine of STENOIT domain. The parameter *"interfaces"* must be adjusted according to need.

We now join the domain as seen in Chapter 8.

```
sudo net rpc join -S SBS -U administrator
```

after entering the password we should see the message:

```
Joined domain STENOIT.
```

Now it will be possible to use the *winbind* utility to get a user list:

```
wbinfo -u
```

or a group list:

```
wbinfo -g
```

Squid

To properly configure Squid we must change the *ldap* helper with *ntlm* by replacing the following 3 lines:

```
auth_param basic program /usr/lib/squid3/squid_ldap_auth \
                -b "ou=Users,dc=stenoit,dc=com" \
                -v3 -f "uid=%s" -h localhost

auth_param basic children 5
auth_param basic credentialsttl 30 minutes
```

with:

```
auth_param ntlm program /usr/bin/ntlm_auth \
                --helper-protocol=squid-2.5-ntlmssp

authenticate_ip_ttl 9 hour
auth_param ntlm children 20
```

and assign the user *proxy* to the *winbindd_priv* group:

```
sudo gpasswd -a proxy winbindd_priv
```

The other parameters remain unchanged, the working principle does not change.

Windows Active Directory Domain Controller

Now let's see, alternatively, how to configure the system if we need to use Windows ADS as authentication server.

Samba configuration

We have already seen how to do this, it is a member server, then do the steps
we have already learned in Chapter 4 where authentication is addressed with an
external LDAP server. We have to be discarded, however, the option *Likewise-
Open* and use the *Kerberos+Samba+Winbind* trio.

If we executed properly the configuration and the join to ADS domain, it will
be possible to use the winbind utility and to obtain the user list:

```
wbinfo -u
```

or the group list:

```
wbinfo -g
```

Squid

To properly configure Squid we have to do two changes. The first is the same
one we saw just above, we change the *ldap* helper with the *ntlm*, by replacing
the following 3 lines:

```
auth_param basic program /usr/lib/squid3/squid_ldap_auth \
                -b "ou=Users,dc=stenoit,dc=com" \
                -v3 -f "uid=%s" -h localhost

auth_param basic children 5
auth_param basic credentialsttl 30 minutes
```

with:

```
auth_param ntlm program /usr/bin/ntlm_auth \
                --helper-protocol=squid-2.5-ntlmssp

authenticate_ip_ttl 9 hour
auth_param ntlm children 20
```

The second thing to do is to change the program called by the directive
external_acl_type, which becomes:

```
external_acl_type win_group protocol=2.5
                %LOGIN /usr/lib/squid3/wbinfo_group.pl
```

(I remember once again that **what is written must be on a single line**) and its
ACL as follows:

```
acl internetfull external win_group internet
```

Even here remember to assign to the user proxy to *winbindd_priv* group:

```
sudo gpasswd -a proxy winbindd_priv
```

The other parameters remain unchanged, the working principle does not
change.

Test script

Winbind maintains a cache of local domain users and groups. If we require that the amendment to the list of members of the Internet group is implemented immediately, we must delete the cache and restart the service. To simplify the process we create a small bash script called *"internetuser"* who performs these steps and, using the same program that external acl (*wbinfo_group.pl*) uses, check that the specified user is a member of the group.

```
sudo nano /usr/bin/internetuser
```

We write the following:

```
# internetuser
# Clear winbind cache e show if user
# is member of ADS group

if [ $# = 0 ]
  then
    echo "use: internetuser <username>"
    exit;
  else
  /etc/init.d/winbind stop
  rm /var/cache/samba/netsamlogon_cache.tdb
  /etc/init.d/winbind start
  echo "$1 internet" | /usr/lib/squid3/wbinfo_group.pl -d
fi;
```

Remember to make the script executable:

```
sudo chmod +x /usr/bin/internetuser
```

Testing operations

We test the functioning of the system described by creating the group "Internet" and adding the user "user1" as a member. If the Domain Controller is Samba doing so:

```
sudo netgroupadd internet
```

assign the test user "user1" to the group:

```
sudo netgroupmod -a user1 internet
```

Otherwise, we use Microsoft tools, and on Proxy Server check/enable the changes immediately with the script we created earlier:

```
sudo internetuser user1
```

which should return at the end a result like this:

```
Sending OK to squid
OK
```

if it is OK, or:

```
Sending ERR to squid
ERR
```

if not.

Remove the NAT configuration from Firewall:

```
sudo nano /etc/shorewall/masq
```

commenting on the line:

```
#INTERFACE SOURCE ADDRESS
#eth0      eth1
```

so we are sure that is not possible to access to Internet except that through our proxy.

Reload the Squid3 configuration.

```
sudo squid3 -k reconfigure
```

Now we set in on user browser as server proxy the *sbs.stenoit.com* address on *port 3128* and check if everything works properly.

Transparent Proxy

As already mentioned, the role of the Transparent Proxy is to intercept every request (like HTTP) in the users' workstations, and then redirect it to our Squid Proxy that undertake all the necessary functions (simple content filtering rather than caching). But be careful: the traffic interception is performed by the Firewall, Squid performs only the proxy tasks.

Forcing to use the client-side proxy is transparent to the user and the administrator is relatively certain to control the HTTP traffic for all stations it manages.

Before choosing a solution of this type, however, we must know one important limitation: using the Transparent Proxy **we can not use any authentication type previously seen**.

Nevertheless, we see how to do in our small installation when we have the Proxy and Firewall on the same machine, so the configuration is quite simple:

Edit the Shorewall configuration file:

```
sudo nano /etc/shorewall/rules
```

and add the following:

```
#ACTION   SOURCE   DEST     PROTO   DEST      SOURCE    ORIGINAL
#                                   PORT(S)   PORT(S)   DEST
REDIRECT  loc      3128     tcp     www       -         !192.168.30.0/24
```

Similar in concept to what we saw in Chapter 9 which deals with SMTP traffic. For the purpose of example we have defined that we will not pass through the proxy requests to the network 192.168.30.x.

Do not forget:

```
sudo shorewall restart
```

to activate the new setting.

WPAD protocol

The Transparent Proxy does not allow us to achieve the desired objective. We need to use an alternative method to automatically configure clients and, at the same time, be able to use authentication.

WPAD (*Web Proxy Autodiscovery Protocol*), developed by a group of software companies (Inktomi, Microsoft, RealNetworks, Sun Microsystems), was just created for this purpose, that is to allow the end user maximum transparency for the configuration of his own browser.

The principle is very simple: the browser that implements this protocol begins its investigation by querying its DNS research, in our case, the host *wpad.stenoit.com*. When a record that matches that name (if any) is found, the browser loads an auto-configuration, the file that corresponds to the following URL:

```
http://wpad.stenoit.com/wpad.dat
```

Once we have created this file and put it in the root of our web server, the browser will execute the directives contained in this Javascript that, in our case, configure the browser to use our Proxy. Now we see how to obtain this result.

DNS configuration

We start by creating the alias on the DNS. If we are using *dnsmasq* just do this:

```
sudo nano /etc/dnshosts
```

adding *wpad*.

```
192.168.20.1 sbs mail wpad stenoit.com
```

later remember to restart the service:

```
sudo /etc/init.d/dnsmasq restart
```

If instead we are using *bind & dhcpd*, we can use our *dnsedit* command. More information can be found in the Chapter 5.

wpad.dat creation

Create the javascript files needed for auto-configuration:

```
sudo nano /var/www/wpad.dat
```

and add the following:

```
function FindProxyForURL( url, host )
  {
  if (dnsDomainIs( host, "www.stenoit.com" ))
     return "PROXY sbs.stenoit.com:3128; " + "DIRECT";
  if( isPlainHostName( host ) ||              // without domain
      dnsDomainIs( host, "stenoit.com" ) || // local domain
      shExpMatch( url, "https*" ) ||          // secure protocols
      shExpMatch( url, "snews*" ) )
    return "DIRECT";
  else
    return "PROXY sbs.stenoit.com:3128; " + "DIRECT";
  }
```

If the client browser requests an internal address (ie not specify the domain name) or the domain is *"stenoit.com"* or even secure URL (*https*) is requested, *wpad.dat* configures your browser with direct access without going through the proxy (DIRECT parameter), otherwise configure the browser to use *"sbs.stenoit.com:3128"*.

For didactic purposes we have introduced here a particular case. The company's web site (*www.stenoit.com*) is not in our network but at our internet hosting provider. So while the domain is always *stenoit.com*, we want that the browser is also directed to our proxy.

Browser

Now we just have to configure the users' browser, so that they use the automatic proxy configuration. We should probably do it manually by accessing the browser network settings selecting:

```
"Auto-detect proxy settings for this network"
```

or something like that.

Traffic control with the firewall

With the Proxy feature we could think to leave the NAT disabled, forcing all users to go to internet through Squid and its authentication.

However, Squid does not support all protocols and we need some software that may require, to function properly, a direct access to the Internet.

Let's see here, using Shorewall, three simple examples to use as guideline to solve this problem without having to provide our users with unrestricted access to the Internet.

First re-enable the NAT:

```
sudo nano /etc/shorewall/masq
```

uncomment the second line:

```
#INTERFACE SOURCE ADDRESS
eth0    eth1
```

Now again all can access the internet in an unconditional way.

Enabling the protocols

We can instruct Shorewall so that only certain protocols are enabled to pass through the firewall. In Chapter 6 we specify this rule in /etc/shorewall/policy:

```
#SOURCE DEST POLICY LOG LEVEL LIMIT:BURST
loc    net  ACCEPT
```

with which we allow all traffic between your internal network *(loc)* and internet *(net)*. If we disable these rules, then **we have to manually handle each protocol** in /etc/shorewall/rules configuration file. For example:

In /etc/shorewall/policy we disable the traffic that goes through the firewall and save in the log file the access attempts *(info)*:

```
loc    net   REJECT    info
```

If we now try to navigate with the browser on the internet without proxy, in the log file, viewable with the command:

```
shorewall show log
```

we'll see something like this:

```
loc2net:REJECT:IN=eth1 OUT=eth0 SRC=192.168.20.10 DST=65.55.21.250 LEN=48
```

That indicates an attempt of violation of the rule *loc2net* from host with IP 192.168.20.10.

Now, by enabling the HTTP traffic to /etc/shorewall/rules as follows:

```
HTTP/ACCEPT    loc      net
```

we enable hosts to navigate freely, because what is indicated in /etc/ shorewall/rules overwrites the default policy set in /etc/shorewall/policy. Likewise, then, we will enable each protocol:

```
FTP/ACCEPT      loc       net
POP3/ACCEPT     loc       net
IMAP/ACCEPT     loc       net
```

by listing all those accepted. This is the best approach, but needs more time and effort because we know the needs of users, and with the help of the log file to identify and resolve problems that arise.

Alternatively, we could work on the other hand leaving all traffic enabled and disabling only protocols that do not wish to be used. In this case the file */etc/shorewall/policy* remains unchanged allowing all traffic, then in */etc/shorewall/rules* we disable the protocols not allowed. For example, if we want to deny only the internet browsing:

```
HTTP/REJECT     loc       net
```

Now network users can, for example, use FTP but they won't be able to browse the Internet without the authentication provided by Proxy.

Allow only specific hosts

After having blocked HTTP traffic to force our members to use the proxy, we suppose now we need to allow only certain specific hosts. To do this we edit again the file */etc/shorewall/rules* and add the bold line (remember that the rules are interpreted in the order they are written):

```
HTTP/ACCEPT    loc:192.168.20.10        net
HTTP/REJECT    loc                      net
```

Now the host with address 192.168.20.10 will be able to access the web directly without the proxy. If we want to enable multiple hosts, we can create a variable that contains a list of the addresses rather than to list them all in the file of rules. We create the file:

```
sudo nano /etc/shorewall/params
```

that Shorewall reads during startup, writing this:

```
ALLOW_IP=192.168.20.10,192.168.20.11,192.168.20.12
```

Then change again the file */etc/shorewall/rules* by putting the variable instead of an IP:

```
HTTP/ACCEPT    loc:$ALLOW_IP           net
HTTP/REJECT    loc                     net
```

This technique assumes you know the host IP address that we want to enable, but since we are in an environment in which they are dynamically assigned by DHCP, it may happen that the host's address changes after a certain period of time .

The ideal solution would be to set the host name rather than its IP, but unfortunately Shorewall does not accept a syntax like this:

```
HTTP/ACCEPT  loc:wks01              net
```

However, we can partially bypass this problem by creating a small bash script that dynamically valorizes a variable in the file /etc/shorewall/params seen before.

First we create a file with a list of hosts to enable:

```
sudo nano /etc/shorewall/allow_host
```

writing one host name per line:

```
wks01
wks02
wks03
```

Now let's create the script:

```
sudo nano /usr/bin/host_ip
```

add this:

```
#!/bin/bash
 first=1;
 for host in $(cat /etc/shorewall/allow_host); do
    IP="`host $host | head -n1 | cut -d" " -f4`";
    if [ $first = 1 ]; then
        allow="$allow$IP";
        first=0;
    else
        allow="$allow,$IP";
    fi
done;
echo $allow;
```

and remembering to make it executable:

```
sudo chmod +x /usr/bin/host_ip
```

the script gets from DNS the list of IP addresses of hosts specified in the configuration file /etc/shorewall/allow_host:

```
192.168.20.40,192.168.20.41,192.168.20.42
```

Now we open again in the editor the file /etc/shorewall/params and add the highlighted line:

```
ALLOW_IP=192.168.20.10,192.168.20.11,192.168.20.12
ALLOW_HOST="`/usr/bin/host_ip`"
```

To complete the work we have to re-edit /etc/shorewall/rules:

```
HTTP/ACCEPT   loc:$ALLOW_IP          net
HTTP/ACCEPT   loc:$ALLOW_HOST        net
HTTP/REJECT   loc                    net
```

The next time you restart Shorewall, evaluating the *params* file for a list of variables, it will implicitly execute the script we have created valorizing the variable *$ALLOW_HOST* with the IP addresses of the hosts listed in the configuration file. In this way from now on, to enable a specific host just put his name in the file and restart the service. *Beware, it isn't dynamic.* If the address of an enabled host changes, to implement the change to the firewall we are always forced to restart Shorewall.

Allow only specific destinations

The last case that we analyze is the possibility to allow users to access only to specific sites. This technique, for example, is useful if we want allow them to access to automatic updates of software that does not support the use of Proxy, or if we want to allow all, without distinction, the updates, for example, the antivirus installed on their desktop.

To do this we must edit again the file */etc/shorewall/rules* by adding (always **before** HTTP/REJECT):

```
HTTP/ACCEPT   loc          net:update.mysoftware.org
HTTP/REJECT   loc          net
```

where *"update.mysoftware.net"* is, of course, the web site to enable.

In a similar way as in the previous section, we can also use a variable created in the */etc/shorewall/params*. For example if we wanted to include a list of destinations, simply insert in the file:

```
ALLOW_DEST=update.mysoftware.net,update.myantivirus.com
```

and edit */etc/shorewall/rules*:

```
HTTP/ACCEPT   loc          net:$ALLOW_DEST
HTTP/REJECT   loc          net
```

Conclusions

We learned how to filter and to limit the outgoing web traffic from our network or through a proxy cache such as Squid or directly through the firewall managed by Shorewall.

There is a deeper difference in practice between the two solutions. Squid operates a control at *user-level*: it means that whatever the host from which, for example, "user1" logs in, Squid ACLs are respected. Shorewall, however, operates a control at *host/IP-level*, with the result that enabling a protocol or service to a particular host, any user that logs on from it will benefit.

With a little study we can extend the concepts and techniques learned in this chapter to other protocols and services in order to provide our users with a safe and efficient working environment.

11

Time Server

We continue with something simple and useful in an SBS: synchronization of date and time in the domain.

The *Network Time Protocol* (NTP), is a client-server protocol to synchronize computer clocks over a network. It is virtually supported by all popular operating systems and so it is a good solution.

In our case we choose a simple and alternative package to the most popular NTPD and learn how to synchronize the date and time on all domain clients.

OpenNTPD

OpenNTPD is a free implementation of the *Network Time Protocol,* easy to configure and use. It allows both to synchronize the local clock with an NTP server, and to distribute the local time on the network.

Installation

We need a single package:

```
sudo apt-get install openntpd
```

Configuration and Start

To configure OpenNTPD we edit its configuration file:

```
sudo nano /etc/openntpd/ntpd.conf
```

We set up the server with which our server needs to synchronize. We can leave the default ones:

```
server 0.debian.pool.ntp.org
server 1.debian.pool.ntp.org
```

```
server 2.debian.pool.ntp.org
server 3.debian.pool.ntp.org
```

Then we set the network interface where the server listens, for the requests from users of our domain:

```
listen on 192.168.20.1
```

We just have to restart the service:

```
sudo /etc/init.d/openntpd restart
```

If needed, we add the rules to our firewall, remembering that the NTP service port is 123.

```
sudo nano /etc/shorewall/rules
```

the directive is:

```
NTP/ACCEPT              loc     $FW
```

Client synchronization

Now that our server has the date and time synchronized with the world, we see how to configure the Windows desktop of STENOIT domain, so that they benefit.

There are two ways: by using the NTP client that we find in the Windows control panel, or with a slight modification to our logon script. In the first case we have to configure one by one all the PCs on your network, in the second we just need a change that can be made directly from the server console.

In fact if we opt for the latter, if we have correctly followed the Chapter 8, we see that we have already done it when we created the perl script responsible for generating custom logon scripts for users. Please ensure that this is true:

```
sudo nano /etc/samba/logon.pl
```

we should see that we have entered the command:

```
# Sync date and time with server
print LOGON "NET TIME \\\\SBS /SET /YES\r\n";
```

that synchronizes the time with the server using NET TIME command. This method has the advantage of working also with the venerable Windows 95 and 98 series.

12

Snapshot Backup

I think that one of the most banal phrases that you can hear in a IT environment is one that says: **"saving data is an important thing!"**. Yet despite this, amazingly it still happens to find people who are convinced of the invincibility of their computer, or other that hiding them behind phrases like **"I don't have time"** or something like that. And I think that nowadays this approach is even more unreasonable than in the past because there are extremely fast and cheap media storage on which to store our data.

So we can not ignore in any way this chapter, where we will learn to use the technique named *Snapshot Backup*, faster, cheaper, and original.

Backup, in fact, can be done in numerous ways. Instead of talking about backup, we should always talk about *"backup strategy"*. The simple copy of the data to another medium is insufficient and even inefficient in terms of cost and security, both as regards the time spent and for the type of the chosen support.

Before we begin let's see how the proposed solution works, from the theoretical point of view.

Backup types

Typically, using a backup strategy means to select the frequency and one of the three methods of data backup: *full, differential* and i*ncremental*.

Full

I think it's easy to understand what I mean with *full*: it consists in creating backup copies of all files in specified folders. If we perform regular backup operation, the choice can be extremely inappropriate, both because of the required time to complete it, and for the unnecessary redundancy of information. In fact, every time we make the backup, we copy everything again, also data not changed since the last saving, wasting time and space on the storage media.

Differential

In the case of *differential* backups, however, the program takes care to verify that the files that need to be re-archived have been changed since the last full backup. The main advantage therefore consists of the drastic decrease of the the time required for restore operations.

Incremental

Incremental backup is appropriate for most situations. In this case we create a backup copy of *all and only those files that were added or changed since the last backup* (full or not). The time that can be saved during the backup is even greater than the *differential* solution, though the latter is much faster if we want to restore the saved data.

Rotating Snapshots

And now, what solution we will use? None of those mentioned, though, objectively, at least in part, it combines the concepts. We will use a technique called **Rotating Snaphshots**, efficient, fast and relatively easy to implement.

The *Snapshot Backups* are a feature of many high-level file servers: they create the illusion of multiple full backups without taking up space and time needed to execute them. Using only the standard Linux commands and *rsync* utility, we can get different hourly, daily, weekly and monthly snapshots, with an efficiency a little bit higher than 2X, on average about twice the space occupied by the data. Do we have 10GB to save? Our backup, occupying just over 20GB, will allow us to pick up even the version of a file of six months ago!

Although there are expensive software on the market that reach, with proprietary file systems, efficiencies slightly higher for 1X, our solution represents a good compromise and, especially, is completely free of charge.

Media

We will use external USB hard disk, cheap, extremely fast and comfortable media, both in backup and restore. Better using at least two disks to swap in the different days.

*N.B. in the server we have used ext3, ext4 or XFS as the file system with extended ACLs. The backup disk **must use the same format** (or ext2 because we do not need journaling), so we can successfully copy the permissions on* *files and directories. We absolutely **cannot use Microsoft NTFS formatted media**.*

Scheduling

In our simple example we will perform three *daily backups* (Monday to Friday on alternate days) and four *weekly backups* (on Saturday). A solution of this type allows us to go back to a specific version of the file on alternate days for a week and for two weeks at intervals of one. We will see, however, that this thing can be changed easily.

In a real case it is better that we perform daily backups at least six and four weekly alternating a couple of physical media: in this way we have two weeks of daily backups and two months of weekly backups .

We try now to understand how and why the snapshot technique works: there are more or less the same principles on which *Apple TimeMachine* and *Linux Fly-Back* are based. Understanding the theory will be easier to manage the backup process in case of trouble and, especially, restore the data.

Soft Link & Hard Link

To begin we must start with two concepts of typical Linux file system: *Soft Links* (called also *symbolic links*) and *Hard Links*. Which is the difference between them?

Soft Link

Normally, the situation is the one we see in figure 1:

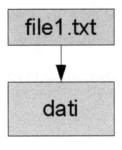

Fig. 1

Where *"file1.txt"* is the name given to the zone *"dati"*. Now let's create a soft link/symbolic link of "file1.txt" with the command:

```
ln -s file1.txt file2.txt
```

What has happened? We can schematize it with the Figure 2:

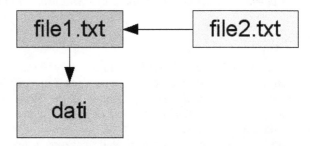

Fig. 2

We have, in effect, created a kind of aliases of *file1.txt* called *file2.txt*. In fact we can now access both the file names with the same result, or almost. Almost refers to the deletion.

In fact, what does it happen if we delete *file2.txt*?

```
rm file2.txt
```

Nothing happens to the data, *file1.txt* continues to exist, we've just deleted the link that we've just created. But if we eliminate file1.txt:

```
rm file1.txt
```

the effects are completely different: *file2.txt* becomes an *orphan* and data (*"dati"* in the figure) are deleted from the file system.

Hard Link

Now we come to the second point. We change slightly the command by removing the *"-s"* flag:

```
ln file1.txt file2.txt
```

in this case we think that you *have created a hard link called "file2.txt" to the file "file1.txt"*, which is conceptually not exactly true. After this *"ln"* command, the situation is:

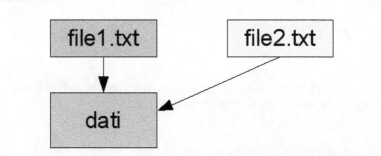

Fig. 3

```
rm file1.txt
```

file2.txt in this case continues to exist and t*he data remain on the file system, accessible through file2.txt.* Thus:

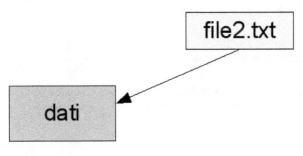

Fig. 4

Look at the figures again, but what is then *file1.txt*? We should have guessed that *is a hard link to the data itself,* which is automatically created when the file (more correctly: *the data file*) was created. Everything, except for soft links and directories, are in fact hard links, this is the *"modus operandi"* of a modern file system.

Between the hard link there is no hierarchical relationship, *file1.txt*, *file2.txt* and all the other possible that point to the same data, have the same importance, **the data that are linked will continue to exist as long as there will be one hard link pointing to them**.

This last phrase in bold, as we shall see, contains the fundamental principle of technology used by the *snapshot backup*. Now we'll see how to use this feature to our advantage.

Backup strategy

We continue in our example, seeing how the backup technique suggested works, just using *cp* and *mv*, commands that are standard in every Linux distribution, and rsync, developed by the creators of Samba and widely available if not installed by default.

So, we use the following strategy:

- ✔ three daily snapshots (daily.0 daily.1 daily.2)
- ✔ two weekly snapshots (weekly.0 weekly.1)

daily snapshots are created on Mondays, Wednesdays and Fridays, the *weekly snapshots* on Saturday. Remember that this is only an example, after that, we will do something better.

We define also the source and destination of the backup:

- ✔ our data are in */samba/share*
- ✔ our backup media is mounted in */mnt/snapshots*

Now we shouldn't give too much attention to the precision of the commands, later we will use the appropriate tools that greatly simplify the job.

We can begin.

daily snapshots

Monday

The first day we don't do much, */mnt/snapshots* is empty and then we have to copy everything (but it **will be the only time**), we can use *rsync*:

```
rsync -a --delete /samba/share /mnt/snapshots/daily.0
```

The following Monday, the situation will be very different as we will see later. Now, however, we have this situation:

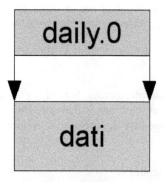

Fig. 5

Nothing difficult to understand.

Wednesday

Our most recent backup will be in *daily.0*, then the second day we start with:

```
cp -al /mnt/snapshots/daily.0 /mnt/snapshots/daily.1
```

Using *cp* with the flag *-al*, the task is very fast: in fact no data are copied, but only the hard links of all the files in *daily.0* in *daily.1* will be created (remember that we cannot create an hard link of a directory). The situation now is this:

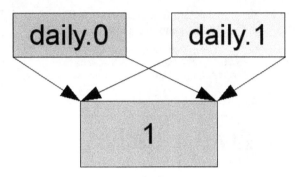

Fig. 6

Practically from both directories we can access to the same data.

Now we run again *rsync* to *daily.0*:

```
rsync -a --delete /samba/share /mnt/snapshots/daily.0
```

What did it happen? Suppose that our backup was 10GB and that between Monday and Wednesday, simplifying, 2GB of data are changed. After this *rsync* the situation will be:

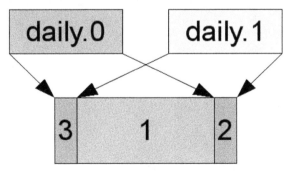

Fig. 7

daily.0 will point data files that are not changed (zone 1 on figure 7) and new files (zone 3), *daily.1* the "shared" data (zone 1) and old files that have changed (zone 2). Rsync (with *--delete* parameter) deletes the destination files no longer present in the source, but due to the properties of the hard links (**the data are not physically removed until there is a hard link refered to them**), in fact remain stored because they are linked by hard links on *daily.1*.

Friday

Let's free space for the new backup that is always performed in *daily.0*, then "shift" the directory, copy hard links and execute rsync again:

```
mv /mnt/snapshot/daily.1 /mnt/snapshot/daily.2
cp -al /mnt/snapshots/daily.0 /mnt/snapshots/daily.1
rsync -a --delete /samba/share /mnt/snapshots/daily.0
```

Now the situation is complicated a little, like so:

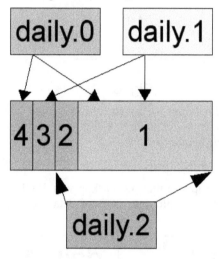

Fig. 8

Simplifying:

- ✔ daily.2 -> 1+2
- ✔ daily.1 -> 1+3
- ✔ daily.0 -> 1+4

I think that the concept makes sense now. Entering in the various backup directory **we have the illusion of having three full backup of three different days**, but, returning to our example, the space occupied **is not 30GB but**

10+2+2=14GB assuming that every two days 10% of the data are changed (this percentage statistically decreases with increasing amount of data). So now I have saved over 50% of disk space, without estimating the significant **time savings** to do the backup.

Next week

But go ahead, what happens when Monday comes back? We said that we keep only three snapshots, therefore we delete the older, "shifts", copy/create hard links and execute again rsync on *daily.0*:

```
rm -rf /mnt/snapshot/daily.2
mv /mnt/snapshot/daily.1 /mnt/snapshot/daily.2
cp -al /mnt/snapshots/daily.0 /mnt/snapshots/daily.1
rsync -a --delete /samba/share /mnt/snapshots/daily.0
```

But now we must ask ourselves: what has been eliminated with the command *rm -rf /mnt/snapshot/daily.2*?

We have seen (Figure 8) that *daily.2* contains hard links pointing to the "zone 1" and "zone 2". By removing the directory in fact **only hard link and the respective data of the "zone 2" are deleted** because the data of the "zone 1" is linked also from *daily.0* and *daily.1* and so they aren't removed (according to the known properties of the hard links that I have repeated many times).

From this point the cycle has started and still continues in this way.

weekly snapshot

We haven't finished. We said we want to keep two weekly backups, *weekly.0* and *weekly.1,* that allow us to restore also data from a couple of weeks earlier.

Saturday

Same as the *daily*, we may think, but no, it's much easier and faster.
We have seen that in the second cycle the older "daily" snapshot (*daily.2*) is deleted, then to make a *weekly* backup just copy its hard links before deleting:

```
cp -al /mnt/snapshots/daily.2 /mnt/snapshots/weekly.0
```

very fast task, which effectively "freezes" the oldest data. In fact at this point the command *rm -rf /mnt/snapshot/daily.2* that runs on the following Monday won't even remove physically the data from the "zone 2" because they are now linked by *weekly.0*.

The next Saturday, we "translate" *weekly.0*, like this:

```
mv /mnt/snapshots/weekly.0 /mnt/snapshots/weekly.1
cp -al /mnt/snapshots/daily.2 /mnt/snapshots/weekly.0
```

the following Saturday again we enter in the infinite loop, which will also include deleting of the oldest weekly snapshot:

```
rm -rf /mnt/snapshot/weekly.1
mv /mnt/snapshots/weekly.0 /mnt/snapshots/weekly.1
cp -al /mnt/snapshots/daily.2 /mnt/snapshots/weekly.0
```

The *weekly* snapshot, so, is extremely fast and does not even have a rsync from the source: it can also be easily scheduled after the daily snapshot on Friday or immediately prior to the Monday one.

That is all. Fast (only one "full" backup, then only incremental/differential), and simple, using commands available at any GNU/Linux system.
Apple TimeMachine uses a very similar mechanism, made more efficient and faster by the fact that while our rsync should still read the entire file system to find modified files, the Apple product uses information stored on the *inode* to find the files to copy or remove, making the process even faster.

Installation

Now that we understand how the suggested technique works, we have to put it into practice.
Instead of wasting time creating their own bash scripts, we will use **rsnapshot**, a great utility written in perl just for this purpose.

Rsnapshot is in the standard Ubuntu repositories,so to install it you just need a simple:

```
sudo apt-get install rsnapshot
```

Configuration

The configuration of *rsnapshot* is quite simple. Just edit the file */etc/rsnapshot.conf* for our needs. The file is well commented and easy to understand after reading the first part of this chapter.

Here is a configuration that might be good for our backup:

```
config_version  1.2
snapshot_root   /mnt/snapshots/
no_create_root  1

cmd_cp          /bin/cp
cmd_rm          /bin/rm
cmd_rsync       /usr/bin/rsync
cmd_logger      /usr/bin/logger

interval        daily   6
interval        weekly  4
```

```
verbose        3
loglevel       3
logfile        /var/log/rsnapshot.log

lockfile       /var/run/rsnapshot.pid

rsync_short_args   -Aarlv
rsync_long_args    --delete --numeric-ids -delete-excluded
link_dest          0

backup   /samba/apps/           sbs/apps
backup   /home/                 sbs/home
backup   /samba/netlogon/       sbs/netlogon
backup   /samba/public/         sbs/public
```

Warning: in the file */etc/rsnapshot.conf* parameters have to be separated with TAB, not with a space!

We now see the most important parameters.

snapshot_root

It indicates the directory where the snapshot is created, that corresponds to where our removable media is mounted.

no_create_root

It's important to set to "1" this directive, because it prevents creating the snapshot if backup media is not mounted.

interval

It defines the types and amount of snapshots that we want to "rotate". There are four possible levels (eg, *hourly, daily, weekly* and *monthly*). In our case we will make six daily and four weekly snapshots. The assigned name defines also the name of the folder that will be created. With:

```
interval daily 6
```

will be created *daily.0, daily.1, daily.2, daily.3, daily.4* and *daily.5*.

rsync_short_args & rsync_long_args

It defines the parameters of *rsync*. They are available with:

```
rsync --help
```

or on its online help.

link_dest

Ubuntu 10.04 is provided with rsync 3.0.7, and so we can set this to "1". This means that it speeds up the backup because it allows, in practice, to skip the command *cp -al*, which creates hard links, as rsync does directly.

backup

How we can imagine, here we define our source and destination of the backup. For example:

```
backup /samba/public/ sbs/public
```

create snapshot of */samba/public* on */mnt/snapshots/daily.0/sbs/public*.

Start snapshot

Now, after having mounted our removable media with:

```
sudo mount -t ext2 /dev/sdb1 /mnt/snapshots
```

we can run *rsnapshot* (or we can schedule it with cron):

```
sudo rsnapshot daily
```

for *daily* backup, or

```
sudo rsnapshot weekly
```

for *weekly*.

Backup notification

Let's go a step further by creating a bash script called *snapback*, which sends the administrator an e-mail with the report of the backup since *rsnapshot* does not provide this functionality directly.

First of all we install, if we haven't already done it, *mailutils,* the package that contains the commands needed to send mail from the command line:

```
sudo apt-get install mailutils
```

And now here's the script:

```
#!/bin/bash
# snapback - Backup with rsnapshot
# by steno 2008-2010

# variables
MAILTO="sbsadmin@stenoit.com"
MAIL="/usr/bin/mail"
logfile="/var/log/rsnapshot.log"
device="/dev/sdb1"
```

```
bckiniz=`date`
bckdel=`date +"%A - %d/%b/%Y"`
# Backup media mounted
volume="/snapshots"

# tmp files
mailfile="/tmp/rsmailfile"
tmplog="/tmp/tmprslog"

# check parameters
if [ $# = 0 ] || ([ $1 != 'daily' ] && [ $1 != 'weekly' ])
 then
   echo "use: snapback {daily|weekly}"
   exit;
fi;

# stores start date and time
bckiniz=`date`;
bckdel=`date +"%A - %d/%b/%Y"`;

# check if media is mounted
if mount | grep "on ${volume} type" > /dev/null
 then
   ismount=1;
 else
   ismount=0;
fi

# If is mounted start snapshot:
if [ $ismount = 1 ]
 then
    # create snapshot :)
    /usr/bin/rsnapshot $1
fi

# store end date and time
bckfine=`date`;

if [ $ismount = 1 ]
 then
   # extract daily log ( the format is : 30/MAR/2010 )
   cat /var/log/rsnapshot.log | tr A-Z a-z | grep `date +"%d/%b/
%Y"` > $tmplog

   # create mail report
   {
    echo "Backup snapshot report - ($1) - "$bckdel;
    echo "";
    echo "Backup start: "$bckiniz;
    echo "Backup end  : "$bckfine;
    echo "";

    # print log rows with "completed" o "error".
    egrep "completed|ERROR" $tmplog;
    echo "--------------------------";
```

```
    echo " Disk use :";
    echo "--------------------------";

    # print backup disk usage
    /usr/bin/rsnapshot du
    echo "";
    /bin/df -h $device
    echo "";
    echo "--------------------------";
    echo "log generated by snapback";
    echo
  } > $mailfile
else
  # Create error email if media is not mounted
  {
    echo "Backup snapshot report - ($1) - "$bckdel;
    echo "";
    echo "Backup start: "$bckiniz;
    echo "Backup end  : "$bckfine;
    echo "";

    echo "-----------------------------------------";
    echo " ERROR !";
    echo "";
    echo " Backup media $volume ";
    echo " is not correctly mounted ";
    echo "-----------------------------------------";
    echo "";
    echo "log genarated by snapback";
    echo
  } > $mailfile
fi

# Send email
$MAIL -s "Backup snapshot report - ($1)" $MAILTO < $mailfile

# Rimove tmp files
rm -f $tmplog
rm -f $mailfile
```

The script, if the backup volume is correctly mounted (*$ismount* = *1*), will run *rsnapshot*, and, at the end, will send an e-mail to *sbsadmin@stenoit.com* like this:

```
Backup snapshot report - (daily) - Thursday - 04/sep/2010

Backup start: sat 4 sep 2010, 00:15:01 CEST
Backup end  : sat 4 sep 1010, 01:41:59 CEST

--------------------------
 Disk usage :
--------------------------
du -csh /snapshots/daily.0/ /snapshots/daily.1/ /snapshots/daily.2/
    /snapshots/daily.3/ /snapshots/daily.4/ /snapshots/daily.5/
    /snapshots/weekly.0/
```

```
114G    /snapshots/daily.0/
3.9G    /snapshots/daily.1/
43G     /snapshots/daily.2/
4.7G    /snapshots/daily.3/
2.8G    /snapshots/daily.4/
2.1G    /snapshots/daily.5/
5.2G    /snapshots/weekly.0/
175G    total


Filesystem          Size  Used Avail Use% Mounted on
/dev/sdb1           232G  175G   46G  80% /mnt/snapshots


------------------------------
log generated by snapback
```

with possible errors, the duration of the backup, disk usage of snapshots (generated by the command *rsnapshot du*) and total disk usage on backup media that
can be obtained manually with command:

```
dh -h /dev/sdb1
```

If the media backup is not mounted we receive an error mail like this:

```
Backup snapshot report - (daily) - Saturday - 04/set/2010
Backup start: sat 4 sep 2010, 14.58.36, CEST
Backup end  : sat 4 sep 2010, 14.58.36, CEST


----------------------------------------
ERROR !

Backup media /snapshots
is not correctly mounted
----------------------------------------

log generated by snapback
```

Scheduling

Now we just have to set up *crontab* to schedule the execution of our backups.
Run the command:

```
sudo crontab -e
```

and set:

```
# backup with rsnapshot
01 00 * * 1 /usr/bin/snapback weekly
15 00 * * 1-6 /usr/bin/snapback daily
```

So on Monday, unlike other days, before the *daily snapshot*, the *weekly snapshot* that saves *daily.5* hard links before its deletion is performed.

Conclusions

The created snapshots are easy to manage, to restore the backup data is a banal copy from disc to disc, the date of creation of the directory (*daily.0, daily.1*, etc.) always tells us the date of the backup.

With adequate media storage we could think also to activate the *monthly* backups, or even *hourly* to have several snapshots in the same day.

In short, everyone should ask:

How important are my files?

That means that the time and expense to make a backup of the data must be proportionate to their value.

13

Instant Messaging Server

In the last years an *Instant Messaging* system has become important also in a company.

The ability to exchange messages in real time is much appreciated, both on a local network and on the Internet, both through a standard PC and with mobile devices, like the latest generation of smartphones.

Very often this kind of service is offered to companies included in expensive and proprietary Groupware solutions (Lotus Notes, Microsoft Exchange, Novell Groupwise, etc..) or even for free (Google, Yahoo, Skype, etc.), but they have the problem that in order to work properly they need to have a permanent internet connection.

So why don't create our own private IM server integrated with our user base on LDAP? Well, that's what we will learn to do in this chapter using Jabber, an open Instant Messaging protocol, free and widely used.

The Babel of formats

Entering into this world we can not bump into a true *Babel of acronyms* and different implementations that are used to accomplish an Instant Messaging service: AIM, ICQ, IRC, MSN, Gtalk, Gadu-Gadu, Yahoo, Sametime, Skype, Jabber. And surely we have forgotten anyone.

We try to find an ideal candidate that meets our goals:

> *I want a free and open messaging system, but without having to compromise, without suffering the advertisement of some kind of*

> *"multinational of messaging", without having to provide private*
> *information about my life, without having to be an adult, or*
> *American, British, French, Russian, without having to provide a*
> *surely spammed e-mail contact, without a bunch of n00b that*
> *they enjoy with their colorful nicknames to send their chains of*
> *every saint they come to mind.*
>
> *I want it to be private and integrated with corporate user*
> *authentication system based on PAM and LDAP, and that*
> *supports messages to off-line users.*

We don't need to worry. With these goals we have wiped out almost all the candidates, with the exception of one: **JABBER**.

The software based on *Jabber/XMPP* protocol is open and standardized, it is also used by Google for its Gtalk service, anyone can create a server. Jabber is installed on thousands of servers spread over the Internet and used by millions of people every day. There are public and private servers that interact with each other, and, in theory, just a single user on any server, and I can communicate instantly with any user anywhere he is registered. This "decentralization" feature make it very similar in effect to a common e-mail service. In addition, and this is a unique feature, through a *gateway* we can also communicate with users on other networks such as *ICQ* and *MSN*.

All this is too much for our needs, we setup a private server, with disabled public registrations, that accepts connections from our private network (and possibly our mobile users) and that use the existing LDAP user database for authentication.

There are different implementations to create the Jabber server side, we will see two alternatives. In the first one we will use *Jabberd2*, the package originally developed in 2000 by the creator of the protocol Jeremie Miller (now at version 2), while in the second part we will use *Openfire*, a cross-platform, user friendly and entirely based on Java solution, very easy to install and manage.

Jabberd2

Let's start with *Jabberd2*, a project that provides open-source server implementation of *XMPP/Jabber* protocols for instant messaging and *XML routing*. The goal of this project is to provide a scalable server, reliable, efficient and extensible to provide a comprehensive set of features, updated with the latest revisions of the protocol.

Jabberd2 is the next generation of the jabberd server rewritten from scratch in C + + for a higher efficiency and scalability.

Installation

We install, so, the version of the package that includes the necessary support to LDAP and MySQL:

```
sudo apt-get install jabberd2
```

LDAP is used for user authentication, MySQL as data storage as an alternative to *sqlite, PostgreSQL* and *BerkeleyDB.*

In addition to the default features provided by Jabberd2, we add the optional *mu-conference* component (*Multi User Conference*, muc) that allows you to do, quite similar to IRC channels, the conversation with more than two users at once.

This component is not present in the standard Ubuntu repositories, so we need to download the source and compile it.

We go to an empty directory, we execute the download:

```
wget http://download.gna.org/mu-conference/mu-conference_0.8.tar.gz
```

and unpack the archive:

```
tar zxvf ./mu-conference_0.8.tar.gz
```

now we enter in the *mu-conference_0.8/src* folder, created by the previous command, and edit the *Makefile* to enable the MySQL support. In this way, *muc* will write *rooms,* which is the name used by Jabberd2 for *chats/confer-ences*, in the database.

To do this, just comment the first line and uncomment the second line:

```
CFLAGS:=$(CFLAGS) -O2 -Wall -I../../lib -I../include `pkg-config
--cflags glib-2.0` -D_JCOMP -D_REENTRANT -DLIBIDN -DHAVE_MYSQL
```

do the same thing with the fourth and fifth line:

```
LIBS:=$(LIBS) -ljcomp -lm `pkg-config --libs glib-2.0` `pkg-
config --libs gthread-2.0` -lexpat -lidn `mysql_config --libs`
```

now we must return to the "father" directory, but before starting the compila-tion we have to install the necessary packages:

```
sudo apt-get install build-essential pkg-config libexpat1-dev
libglib2.0-dev libidn11-dev libmysqlclient15-dev
```

Now we are ready: from *mu-conference_0.8* type:

```
make
```

The compilation is very fast and at the end we copy the executable files in their place by changing its name:

```
cp ./src/mu-conference /usr/sbin/jabberd2-muc
cp ./muc-default.xml /etc/jabberd2/muc.xml
```

Configuration

The configuration of *Jabberd2* is quite complicated, we must pay particular attention to the syntax of its configuration files, typing mistakes is very easy and would undermine the proper working of the service.

Jabberd2 configuration files are in XML format and there is one for each *"component"* (or *"plugin"*, or *"service"*) that we use. We will use four of them, three are directly supplied by Jabberd2, *SM* (Session Manager), *C2S* (Client to Server) and *ROUTER* and the one we've just compiled, *MUC* (Multi User Conference).

Jabberd2 supports several "schemes" for the user authentication and data storage, in this case we will use PAM for authentication (ie LDAP) and a MySQL database to save our chat sessions and the *"roster"* (the contact list) of users.

DNS and server names

First of all we must decide the name of our IM server and make sure that this is resolvable by DNS. In our case we need two new names:

- ✔ *im.stenoit.com* -> chat IM server
- ✔ *rooms.stenoit.com* -> muc IM server for multi-user conference

As we saw in Chapter 5, with *dnsmasq* just put them in */etc/dnshost*.

```
192.168.20.1 sbs im rooms mail stenoit.com
```

In this way, the DNS will resolve our new host names. Also remember to change the DNS table of our provider if we want to access the service from outside.

MySQL

In Chapter 7 we have installed MySQL, we must now create the tables and database for Jabberd2. To do this a convenient SQL dump is provided, that does this automatically.

Unpack the file:

```
sudo gzip -d /usr/share/doc/jabberd2/db-setup.mysql.gz
```

Connect to the database server:

```
sudo mysql -uroot -p
```

and run it by creating the database "jabberd2" with necessary tables:

```
\. /usr/share/doc/jabberd2/db-setup.mysql
```

Add *muc* tables. The file path of the dump varies depending on where we've downloaded/compiled *muc*, in our case is the user's home *sbsadmin*:

```
use jabberd2
\. /home/sbsadmin/mu-conference_0.8/mu-conference.sql
```

Now we create a user *"jabber"* with password *"pwdjab"* that will be used by Jabberd2 to access the database:

```
GRANT ALL PRIVILEGES ON jabberd2.* TO 'jabber'@'localhost'
IDENTIFIED BY 'pwdjab' WITH GRANT OPTION;
```

with *"quit"* command we can now leave the MySQL interface.

PAM

Configure *PAM* providing the necessary rules for the authentication by creating the file:

```
sudo nano /etc/pam.d/jabberd
```

and write this:

```
#%PAM-1.0
auth            sufficient      pam_ldap.so
auth            required        pam_unix.so nullok
account         sufficient      pam_ldap.so
account         required        pam_unix.so
```

openSSL

To encrypt the conversation we create an SSL key. This step is not required for the basic operation of the service, but should give more security, especially if we want to enable mobile users to connect from the Internet.

Remember that the key generated in this way is *self-signed*, thus not provided by an official Certification Authority. This usually produces a warning message, that we can easily turn off, during client connection.

Key generation

To generate the key we go to */etc/jabberd2* and type the command:

```
sudo openssl req -new -x509 -newkey rsa:1024 -days 3650 -keyout pkey.pem -out imkey.pem
```

We will request a *passphrase* for the private key (don't forget it!) and then public information about our fake *Certification Authority*. The really important thing is to enter the *Common Name*, which should correspond to our domain. In our example *im.stenoit.com*.

Now we remove the *passphrase* from our private key (by typing the passphrase just created):

```
sudo openssl rsa -in pkey.pem -out pkey.pem
```

we combine public and private key in a single file and remove the private key that is no longer required:

```
sudo cat pkey.pem >> imkey.pem
sudo rm pkey.pem
```

and finally we give the correct permissions to the newly created key:

```
sudo chown jabber /etc/jabberd2/imkey.pem
sudo chmod 640 /etc/jabberd2/imkey.pem
```

Well. Our certificate is ready.

Jabberd2

So we now configure our Jabberd2. Each component has its own XML configuration file in */etc/jabberd2*.

Session Manager - sm.xml

The file *sm.xml* configure the Session Manager component, a software layer between the Router (see below) and the external components (S2S, C2S, MUC ...). Now we highlight the points on which we need to work.

Server name

The name must be valid, resolved by DNS.

```
<!-- Our ID on the network. Users will have this as the domain part of
     their JID. If you want your server to be accessible from other
     Jabber servers, this ID must be resolvable by DNS.s
     (default: localhost) -->
  <id>im.stenoit.com</id>
```

User and password for Router

We need to specify username and password to connect to the *Router* component of Jabberd2. Let's change the default password "*secret*" with "*pwdjab*", the important thing is that we use, then, always the same:

```
<!-- Username/password to authenticate as -->
    <user>jabberd</user>        <!-- default: jabberd -->
    <pass>pwdjab</pass>         <!-- default: secret -->
```

SSL certificate

We have already created a certificate, here we must now specify its path:

```
<!-- File containing a SSL certificate and private key to use when
     setting up an encrypted channel with the router. If this is
     commented out, or the file can't be read, no attempt will be
     made to establish an encrypted channel with the router. -->

  <pemfile>/etc/jabberd2/imkey.pem</pemfile>
```

Database

We want to use MySQL as storage (the default is the Berkeley DB) by setting it as a driver. Also enter username and password used by Jabberd2 to access to the database:

```
<!-- Storage database configuration -->
  <storage>
    <!-- By default, we use the MySQL driver for all storage -->
    <driver>mysql</driver>

<!-- Database username and password -->
    <user>jabber</user>
    <pass>pwdjab</pass>
```

Administration user

Although it is not required, we define the user that will be administrator. Jabberd2 has a complex ACLs (*Access Control List*) configuration:

```
<!-- The JIDs listed here will get access to all restricted
     functions, regardless of restrictions further down -->
  <acl type='all'>
    <jid>sbsadmin@im.stenoit.com</jid>
  </acl>
```

Server identity

Enter the name of our IM Server:

```
<!-- Service identity. these specify the category, type and name
     of this service that will be included in discovery information
     responses. -->
  <identity>
    <category>server</category>      <!-- default: server -->
    <type>im</type>                  <!-- default: im -->
    <name>StenoIT IM server</name>   <!-- default: Jabber IM server -->
  </identity>
```

Auto-create users

In our case, PAM authenticates users, but the user must also exist on the jabberd2 database. For this reason, then, we must ensure that users are *automatically created* on the first access:

```
<!-- User options -->
  <user>

    <!-- By default, users must explicitly created before they can start
         a session. The creation process is usually triggered by a c2s
         component in response to a client registering a new user.
```

```
Enableing this option will make it so that a user create will be
triggered the first time a non-existant user attempts to start
a session. This is useful if you already have users in an
external authentication database (eg LDAP) and you don't want
them to have to register. -->
```

```
<auto-create/>
```

Client to Server component - c2s.xml

As the name would indicate, this component controls the communication between server and jabber clients. Its configuration is set up with the file *c2s.xml*.

User and password for Router

Also this component must interface with the Jabberd2 Router, then specify the same user and password as before:

```
<!-- Username/password to authenticate as -->

    <user>jabberd</user>      <!-- default: jabberd -->
    <pass>pwdjab</pass>       <!-- default: secret -->
```

Server identification

Even here we must specify the server name resolved by the DNS in the file *sm.xml*. Moreover, in a public IM Server, we usually allow users to register them, but in our case we must remove the attribute *"register-enable"* to disable this feature since our users are already in our LDAP tree.

We pay attention also to attribute *"realm"*: using PAM authentication we have to set an empty string, otherwise the system would attempt to authorize the username with the server ID. In practice, if the user was *"projects1"*, PAM, incorrectly, try to find a user called *"projects1@im.stenoit.com"*.

The attributes *"pemfile"*, *"test-mode"* and *"require-STARTTLS"* indicate that we want to establish a secure connection with clients.

```
<id realm=''
    pemfile='/etc/jabberd2/imkey.pem'
    verify-mode='7'
    require-starttls='true'
    instructions='Specifica utente e password per collegarsi'
>im.stenoit.com</id>
```

SSL certificate

As above. Please note that we have to indicate it in two places, for the router and for the clients that use the old protocol.

```
<!-- File containing a SSL certificate and private key to use when
     setting up an encrypted channel with the router. If this is
     commented out, or the file can't be read, no attempt will be
     made to establish an encrypted channel with the router. -->
    <pemfile>/etc/jabberd2/imkey.pem</pemfile>
```

```
<!-- Local network configuration -->
    <pemfile>/etc/jabberd2/imkey.pem</pemfile>
```

User authentication

Now we define the authentication scheme for users: we said that we will use PAM, the alternatives are *db* (Berkeley), *MySQL* or *PostgreSQL*:

```
<!-- Authentication/registration database configuration -->
  <authreg>
    <!-- Backend module to use -->
    <module>pam</module>
```

Router component - router.xml

The *Router* is the most important component: it is the *backbone* of the Jabberd2 server. Through it the various components communicate with each other to complete their function. Its configuration is done with two files.

router-users.xml

Define user and password (in our case only one) with which the other components are connected to the router.

```
<!-- This is the list of known router users, and their authentication
     secrets. Access control is done via the settings in router.xml -->
<users>
  <user>
    <name>jabberd</name>
    <secret>pwdjab</secret>
  </user>
</users>
```

router.xml

Once again, the password:

```
<!-- Shared secret used to identify legacy components (that is,
     "jabber:component:accept" components that authenticate using
       the "handshake" method). If this is commented out, support for
       legacy components will be disabled. -->

  <secret>pwdjab</secret>
```

and SSL certificate path:

```
<!-- File containing a SSL certificate and private key for
     client connections. If this is commented out, connecting
       components will not be able to request a SSL-encrypted
       channel. -->

    <pemfile>/etc/jabberd2/imkey.pem</pemfile>
```

Server to Server component - s2s.xml

If, as we decided before, our server is private, we do not need this component. It handles communications between servers that would allow us, if we want, to enter the Jabber universe.

Be careful, "private" does not mean that we can't connect from the internet to our server, but it just means that with an account set up here we can't communicate directly with a generic jabber user registered, for example, on *jabber-.linux.com* and vice versa. By logging on to our server we can only chat with other users on the same.

However, if we want to interact with other users on other Jabber servers (eg *Google Gtalk* users, very common on mobile devices like Blackberry and Android), we should enable and configure this component. The structure is very similar to other files, we must provide the certificate path, the password for the router and the resolver (see below).

Resolver - resolver.xml

This component is linked to the previous *s2s.xml* and it is required only if we want to use the communication between Jabber servers. Looking at the file we will see once again a common structure to specify password for the router and ssl certificate.

Multi User Conference - muc.xml

As we have seen, this is not a component of standard Jabberd2, but it is interesting because it extends the functionality allowing us to communicate with multiple users with a mechanism similar to the IRC channels (here called *rooms*).

First of all we have to manually create the directory where we save the rooms:

```
sudo mkdir /etc/jabberd2/rooms
```

muc.xml

The configuration is done with the file *muc.xml* that is very similar to the earlier ones we saw.

Let's start with the server name (must be resolvable by DNS):

```
<name>rooms.stenoit.com</name> <!--the jid of your component -->
<host>rooms.stenoit.com</host> <!--should be the same as above-->
```

The usual password for the router and the usual ssl certificate path (to be added):

```
<secret>pwdjab</secret>

<!-- secret shared with the jabber server -->
<pemfile>/etc/jabberd2/imkey.pem</pemfile>
```

And various other parameters such as spool directories created before, the PID, the location of log files and the user administrator:

```
<spool>/etc/jabberd2/rooms</spool>

<!-- directory containing the rooms data -->

<logdir>/var/log/jabberd2</logdir>
<!-- directory containing the debug log
  (the file is called mu-conference.log) →
<pidfile>/var/run/jabberd2/mu-conference.pid</pidfile>

<sadmin>
  <user>sbsadmin@im.stenoit.com</user>
</sadmin>
```

to end up with the parameters for the connection to the database:

```
<mysql>
  <user>jabber</user>
  <pass>pwdjab</pass>
  <database>jabberd2</database>
  <host>localhost</host>
</mysql>
```

We have finished.

Service start

Multiples jabbed2 services are driven by startup files that are located in:

```
/etc/jabberd2/component.d
```

one for each plugin.

```
/etc/jabberd2/component.d/10router
/etc/jabberd2/component.d/20resolver
/etc/jabberd2/component.d/30sm
/etc/jabberd2/component.d/40s2s
/etc/jabberd2/component.d/50c2s
```

We disable *s2s* and *resolver*, which in our case are not needed, and enable the new *muc* creating the variable. To do this just edit the file:

```
sudo nano /etc/default/jabberd2
```

and in our case will be:

```
RESOLVER_RUN=0
S2S_RUN=0
```

```
MUC_RUN=1
```

We create, now, the startup file for the *muc* service that, since we installed it manually, does not have it. To do it simply duplicate an existing one:

```
sudo cp /etc/jabberd2/component.d/50c2s /etc/jabberd2/component.d/60muc
```

and modify it by setting the first line with:

```
NAME=muc
```

and, a little below, the line with the test variable:

```
# exit now if we are not ment to run
test "${MUC_RUN}" != 0 || exit 0
```

Well. Now just restart the service:

```
sudo /etc/init.d/jabberd2 restart
```

Internet access

To allow access to our messaging server to mobile users who connect through the Internet, we need to include specific rules on our firewall. We can use an Shorewall *macro* by entering in */etc/shorewall/rules*:

```
Jabberd(ACCEPT)          net      $FW
JabberPlain(ACCEPT)      net      $FW
JabberSecure(ACCEPT)     net      $FW
```

Openfire

After the complex, but instructive, configuration needed to Jabberd2, rewind the tape and dedicate ourselves to an alternative server solution, but always open-source, developed in java. *Openfire* is, unlike what we saw earlier, incredibly easy to install and administer, while offering security and performance. The software is developed by *Igniterealtime*, an open source community with end users and developers around the world who are interested in creating an innovative and open standards for corporate *"Real Time Collaboration"*. A demonstration of the value of the project just think that the Instant Messaging part of *VMware Zimbra*, a modern and innovative open-source system for the messaging and collaboration, alternative to products like Microsoft Exchange, comes directly from Openfire.

Installation

Since Openfire is developed in Java, so we first need to install the runtime environment of Sun/Oracle in the version 6. Ubuntu now uses the default OpenJDK java implementation which in this case does not go well. We enable, therefore, the "partner" repository and install the official Java implementation:

```
sudo nano /etc/apt/sources.list
```

and uncomment (remove "#") the following lines:

```
deb http://archive.canonical.com/ lucid partner
deb-src http://archive.canonical.com/ lucid partner
```

Now update package list and install the JRE from Sun/Oracle:

```
sudo apt-get update
sudo apt-get install sun-java6-jre
```

accepting, of course, the license conditions and any configuration changes that are proposed.

Download directly from *Igniterealtime* site the binary on *deb* format, at the time of this writing is version 3.7.0. Please note the following command that *must always be on one line*:

```
wget http://www.igniterealtime.org/downloadServlet?
filename=openfire/openfire_3.7.0_all.deb -O openfire_3.7.0_all.deb
```

If there are problems with the command go directly to the site and proceed with the download. Once finished, we have to install it:

```
sudo dpkg -i openfire_3.7.0_all.deb
```

Service start

At the end the service starts automatically. If we need to restart just type the simple command:

```
sudo /etc/init.d/openfire restart
```

Configuration

Openfire is quite flexible in its configuration options, it can easily be installed as a standalone server with no other requirement: it has its own internal database and its system of authentication. In our case, however, we will go further, because we want to use MySQL database as the basic service and, of course OpenLDAP or Active Directory as an alternative system for authenticating users, in line with what has been proposed in this book. Let's see how to reach our target point by point.

MySQL

We have already installed MySQL in Chapter 7, now we must create a database and its user that can be used by our IM service.

We start from the database, named *"openfire",* typing, when requested, the password that we defined in Chapter 7 during MySQL installation:

```
mysqladmin create openfire -u root -p
```

and end with the user, with the same name as the database, with password *"openpwd".* Connect to the server:

```
mysql -u root -p
```

create the user:

```
GRANT ALL PRIVILEGES ON openfire.* TO 'openfire'@'localhost'
IDENTIFIED BY 'openpwd' WITH GRANT OPTION;
```

and exit:

```
exit
```

LDAP Authentication

We want that also the users of the IM service are integrated with the corporate LDAP tree. As we have seen many times in this book, we have two possibilities represented by the OpenLDAP or Active Directory. Let's see first how to prepare the environment.

OpenLDAP

To prevent that all the entire LDAP tree becomes involved, we restrict the access of *Openfire* to a single OU, in our case this:

```
ou=Users,dc=stenoit,dc=com
```

we then create a new OU inside it that contains the special groups that are then used by Openfire.

To simplify things we use *phpldapadmin* installed in Chapter 7. From a PC on the network we point our browser to:

```
http://sbs.stenoit.com/phpldapadmin
```

and we see:

insert password (in our example *ldappwd*) and we should see the full LDAP tree:

Now open the *ou=Users* and create an *Organizational Unit (OU)* called *Open-fireGroups*. Inside we create *Posix Group (cn)* and the users that want to provide the IM service.

At the end we should get something like this:

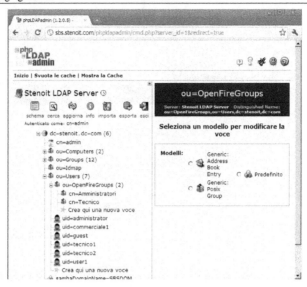

phpldapadmin is quite intuitive and we should not encounter any problems in this phase.

Active Directory

Here, as in the case of OpenLDAP, you should create a separate structure to prevent Openfire also read user and group management of the default domain. For example, in creating an *OU=SBS* dedicated to the purpose:

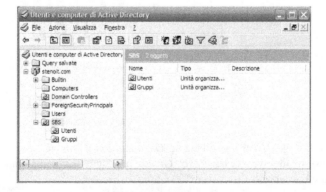

Openfire read users and groups only on the inside of this organizational unit.

Openfire

Now start configuring Openfire itself. From our browser we access its admin interface:

```
http://sbs.stenoit.com:9090
```

the first time we will be asked a series of parameters.

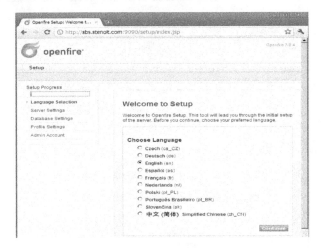

We begin by choosing the appropriate language. Press *"Continue"*.

In the *"Server Settings"* set the name of our server, *im.stenoit.com*. Remember that the name *must be resolved by our DNS*, otherwise an error is displayed at the end of the setup process. We leave unchanged the ports used as well.

When done, press again *"Continue"*.

Now we must set the configuration of the database used by Openfire: after selecting *"Standard Database Connection"* choose *MySQL* as driver, and fill the fields as shown, also specifying the correct password *"openpwd"*.

The other possible option is *"Embedded Database"*, which uses, as its name suggests, the internal Openfire database. Since this does not have a low level administrative interface, it is better, if possible, to use an open, standard and well documented database as MySQL, which makes them easier to maintenance and backup.

Press *"Continue"* again.

Now we must set the configuration for user profiles, groups and their passwords. Leaving aside the *"Clearspace Integration"*, which doesn't interest us here, there are two choices:

"Default" uses the database set in the previous point and allows complete freedom of creation and management of users and groups through the Openfire

administrative interface. If the IM service is marginal and should not be integrated with LDAP, it might be a viable option.

"Directory Server (LDAP)" instead, integrates Openfire, as already indicated, with an external authentication system like OpenLDAP or Active Directory. The obvious advantage here is that we can use the same user/password of the other business services. The disadvantage is that this choice puts limits on the management of users, groups and the "rosters" (contact list) using the Openfire administrative interface. Since each user must exists in the LDAP, we can't, for example, add users that are not part of our organization and enable the free registration.

However we have already decided that this will be our choice, and then after the selection, we will ask the LDAP parameters:

Now we see both cases.

OpenLDAP

If the server type will be *"OpenLDAP"*, insert the following parameters:

Host	localhost
Base DN	ou=Users,dc=stenoit,dc=com

Administrator DN	cn=admindc=stenoit,dc=com

Only users within the *"Base DN"* become Openfire users.
We can, before continuing, testing if the parameters are correct with the button "Test Settings".

On the next page, *"User Mapping"*, leave the default values. Even here we can test if working before continue with the *"Group Mapping"*. Here we must set only the field *"Member Field"* with *memberUid* value. Openfire now will find the list of groups in the *"OU"* that we created before, obtaining also the list of users who are members.

Here's what we see in the mask. Even here we can and must test its working. If we press the button *"Test settings"*, we should get the list of groups created in the OU *"OpenfireGroups"* and the number of its members.

Active Directory

If the server type will be "Active Directory", insert the following parameters:

Host	sbswin.stenoit.com
Base DN	ou=SBS,dc=stenoit,dc=com
Administrator DN	cn=administrator,cn=users,dc=stenoit,dc=com

Even here we can test if it works.

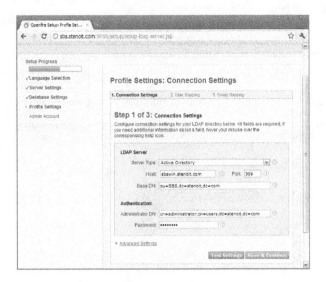

On the next page about the *"User Mapping"* set *"sAMAccountName"* in the *"Username Field"* and *"{displayName}"* in the *"Name"* of the *"Profile Field"* as shown below:

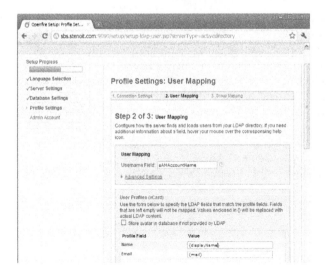

On the next screen, *"Group Mapping"*, we can accept what has being proposed by default.

The last settings does not depend on what type of LDAP server we've chosen first. We need to set what are the account with administrator privileges. We can add *"administrator"* user or any other that is a member of the correct Organization Unit.

At this point we can complete the configuration phase.

If everything is OK we should see the screen that indicates that the setup process is completed successfully inviting us to connect to the administrative console. Let's do it.

Remember that this is not a complete guide to Openfire, now we will restrict ourselves to some basic notions, like the configuration of the groups in order to easily set the *"roster"* of users and the installation of plugins available online to expand its functionality. The management is fairly intuitive, but if there are any problems we can contact the support forums available online.

Let's see how to automatically populate the user list. Login to administration interface and go in the *"Users/Groups"* section. We should see something like this:

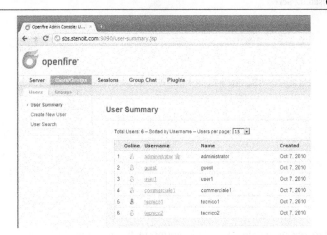

The yellow star indicates the user logged into the administrative section, the green small icon next to "*tecnico1*" indicates that the user is logged into chat. Remember that we chose to use OpenLDAP (or Active Directory) for authentication, and then we can not create new users and groups from here. In fact, clicking on "*Create New User*" we get an error message:

To create new users we must use the tools provided by LDAP as seen in Chapter 8.

If you now select "*Groups*" section we should see the following:

Those we see aren't the standard groups in the domain, but are users thet we have just created with *phpldapadmin* into *OU=OpenfireGroups*. These groups are the same ones that appear in the contact list (roster) of IM users.

For example, we click on the group *"Tecnico"*:

and select *"Enable contact list group sharing"*, *"Share group with additional users"* and *"All users"*. In this simple way we have created the contact list of users! In fact, if we select now *"Users"* followed by *"tecnico1"* and *"Roster"* we see the following:

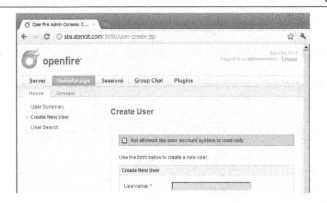

which is the same thing we should do with a jabber client, such as PSI:

Very easy. Such a simplified Roster management with Jabberd2 was virtually impossible to obtain.

Client configuration

After learning how to create a Jabber server, it's the time to dedicate us to the clients side and their integration with our network infrastructure.

At this point, since our server is running and operational, just install and configure any client that supports *XMPP/Jabber* on each PC on the network that we want to enable the IM service.

However, using the File Server discussed in Chapter 8, we can avoid it, being able to centrally manage the deployment of the client and its configuration.

PSI

There are many software client for Jabber, we will use PSI, mainly for the following reasons:

- ✔ Is developed with *QT4*. This means, if you need them, *cross-platform*.
- ✔ Is *mono-protocol*. PSI only supports jabber, and this is good for us, because we don't want that alternative chat types are used.
- ✔ Is *portable*. This means that under Windows, can be used without being installed. This is crucial for us because we will put PSI and its configuration file on a shared folder on the server.
- ✔ Is *complete* and *widespread*. If we look at the list of available clients for Jabber, we see that PSI is one of the most important.

Roster

As we have seen, jabber calls *"Roster"* the list of contacts. If we have chosen *Jabberd2* as server solution, we do not have centralized management capabilities provided instead by Openfire. To mitigate this problem, we can make that every user, *on the first logon*, create their own Roster with a default corporate contact list. To obtain this result we must create a template file and change the Session Manager (sm.xml file):

Let's start from the template, starting with the example:

```
sudo nano /etc/jabberd2/templates/roster.xml
```

here's an excerpt:

```
<!-- This is the roster template. If enabled in sm.xml, new users will
     get this roster by default. -->

<query xmlns='jabber:iq:roster'>
  <item name='Antony' jid='antony@im.stenoit.com' subscription='both'>
    <group>Commercial</group>
  </item>
  <item name='Lucy' jid='lucy@im.stenoit.com' subscription='both'>
    <group>Commercial</group>
  </item>
  <item name='Mike' jid='mike@im.stenoit.com' subscription='both'>
    <group>Projects</group>
  </item> </query>
```

As we can see, the contacts can also be divided into convenient groups. On the first access (remember, *only at first one!*) the user will take this list and will include contacts in its Roster.

In this file we can include all the business contacts, so will not need authorization to communicate with each other through the chat.

Now modify the Session Manager configuration file to ensure that this template is distributed to all our users:

```
sudo nano /etc/jabberd2/sm.xml
```

and then comment out the appropriate section indicating the location of the template file that we have created.

```
<!-- If you defined publish, you should comment <roster> -->
<roster>/etc/jabberd2/templates/roster.xml</roster>
```

Now we just have to restart the service. Unfortunately, as we understand, additions or alterations to the contact list can not be made centrally but independently by each user.

Client installation

This procedure is a little complicated. Having decided to centralize the management of PSI, we must make a preliminary procedure for every user that we are going to enable.

1. Execute the normal installation of PSI on a Windows client that will be used as a template model.
2. Run PSI
3. Create an account (one of those listed on the template *roster.xml*). Remember that users already exist and are stored onto the LDAP, then we have to use *an existing domain user*.
4. Configure PSI as the default seems to be optimal for each user.
5. On account configuration the only thing to which pay attention is the obligatory flag *Ignore SSL warnings* in the *Connection TAB*: otherwise our people will always receive a warning message when connecting to the server, because our SSL certificate is *self signed*.

At this point we should have the model set up and ready for use. The configuration was saved in *c:\documents and settings\<user>\PsiData*.

Now we continue with the configuration:

6. On the server create the directory */samba/apps/psi*, where we will put the client. For Windows users, this path will be *X:\PSI*.
7. Copy the entire contents of *c:\program files\psi* from the PC used to create the model in the *X:\PSI*.
8. Create *x:\psi\psidata* that will contain the users configuration, one separate folder for each user.
9. For every user create a personal folder in this path. The name must match the user name. For example *x:\psi\psidata\user1* for user1.
10. Copy the contents of c:\documents *and settings\<user>\PsiData* just created, in *x:\psi\psidata\user1*
11. Edit the file *x:\psi\psidata\user1\profiles\default\config.xml* and modify the section with *<accounts>* tag to match *user1* data.
12. Repeat points 9-10-11 for each user.

Run client

PSI by default stores the data in the local user profile. Instead, we want centralized configuration on the server. To change the path used by PSI we must define a variable environment called *PSIDATADIR* with the appropriate value.

The easiest way to do this without manual intervention on each host of the network is to use the file *logon.pl* that we created in Chapter 8 to manage customized logon script for each domain user.

So we edit the file:

```
sudo nano /etc/samba/logon.pl
```

create a new variable that contains the messaging service enabled users:

```
$JABBER = "-user1-user2-user3-";
```

and add this rule at the end, remembering that *$ARGV[0]* contains the name of the user who logs on.:

```
# JABBER on PC
if (index($JABBER,"-".lc($ARGV[0])."-") >=0)
  {
    print LOGON "set PSIDATADIR=\\\\SBS\\APPS\\psi\\psidata\\$ARGV[0]\r\n";
    print LOGON "start \\\\SBS\\APPS\\PSI\\PSI.EXE\r\n";
  }
```

At the next domain logon, for every users that are included in the *$JABBER* variable, PSI will be configured and started with the contact list already available. In this way, enable and disable a user is quite simple for the administrator, simply prepare the configuration file and add the user name to the *$JABBER* list.

Let's do it, for example, for *projects1* user:

✔ create *x:\psi\psidata\projects1* by cloning an existing one from another user
✔ set *config.xml* file with *project1* data
✔ add *project1* in the *$JABBER* list in *logon.pl* file
✔ we say to *projects1* to reconnect to the domain.

Well, now *projects1* can start to play with corporate chats.

14

Fax Server

I remember a decade ago (or maybe more) when famous people prophesied the demise of the fax from our offices within the next few years:

"The e-mail will kill the fax, an old-fashioned and outdated method for transmitting information".

I don't think that this is happened, at least in Italy, the country where I live. The reason is trivial, the fax is the cheapest way to certify the identity of the person or company that is sending us something and to get a receipt that confirms the submission of a communication to a recipient.

We see, then, how to install a service for sending and receiving faxes with our server.

Hylafax

When we talk about fax services for Linux, the first thing we think is always *Hylafax*: without any doubt it is the most important player on this platform (and not only) for this kind of service.

Originally developed by SGI, it is a very interesting, powerful and scalable product. It use a client/server protocol very similar to FTP, and if configured properly, we can send and receive faxes using our personal PC without buying any commercial fax machine or software.

Hylafax send fax documents, trying to send them to a predefined number of times (when the first attempts are not successful because of the busy number or other errors). Of course, you can only send files. To send the printed sheets you must first acquire them with a scanner. The solution is therefore very suitable for the delivery of documents or information, but not for the dispatch of signed documents.

You can send all the documents produced by programs that can print, and those who can produce files in Postscript, PDF, or text format.

There are also numerous configurations that allow, for example, to receive a reply when sending a fax via e-mail, attaching, if desired, also the TIFF or PDF of the fax sent.

Hylafax can of course also handle incoming faxes, managing the reply to the call from the remote fax machine, receiving data, and generating a file (defined in many standard formats) that can then be read by users on the network.

It can use multiple phone lines, specifying which dedicate to send and/or receiving faxes, prioritizing, and more.

There are many other possibilities offered by this product, for example:

✔ make a fax broadcasting (ie, send a fax to multiple recipients at one time);
✔ receive faxes by e-mail (attached to mail itself)
✔ send faxes via mail (as attachments)
✔ deliver faxes automatically within our network
✔ automatically print received faxes.
✔ client for Windows, Mac and Linux, and others.

Modem

Obviously we need at least a modem. There are many supported models, internal and external, USB or ISA. However, external serial models are preferable, because they are easier to manage.

Hylafax can use the fax modem class 1, 2, 2.0 and 2.1, which between them have important differences, especially between Class 1 and 2 and the remaining 2.x.

In the class 2, 2.0 and 2.1 modems have a special chip that manages the communication, then the server or computer where the modem is connected is less busy. By contrast the Class 1 modems, however, are generally cheaper and do not contain specific internal hardware for sending faxes. With devices like this, then, is the server that controls the transmission. And if your computer's CPU is running other processes while it is being sent or received a fax message, it is possible that the fax transmission can fail or break.

This makes us understand that if the workload would be heavy on different lines, a good idea is always to use a Class 2, 2.0 and 2.1 modems, or use a dedicated machine with good power. If not, the simple Class 1 are preferable.

Installation

The installation is not difficult. As usual, Hylafax is present in the standard Ubuntu repository and then let's do this:

```
sudo apt-get install hylafax-server hylafax-client
```

Configuration

General

From the console type:

```
sudo faxsetup
```

This command will start the configuration script in which, unless you have special needs, only a few parameters among those requested change. For the others the default settings are good.
We see the most important ones:

```
CountryCode: 0039
```

indicating the country code of Italy. Obviously you have to write the right one for your country.

Our own code number:

```
AreaCode: 02
```

Our telephone number for receiving faxes:

```
FAXNumber: 20304050
```

Ring number before automatic answering in fax reception:

```
RingsBeforeAnswer: 5
```

Enable (*on*) or disable (off) modem speaker:

```
SpeakerVolume: on
```

Fax header:

```
LocalIdentifier: "Stenoit Corporation"
```

Modems

As soon as the general configuration is finished, *faxsetup* automatically starts *faxaddmodem* to configure the first modem.
Later it is possible to configure another modem simply typing:

```
sudo faxaddmodem ttyS0
```

where *ttyS0* indicates, for example, a modem connected to *COM1*, *ttyS1* for *COM2* and so on. Generally, the modem and its features are detected automatically.

The required parameters are practically the same as we saw during the general setup of Hylafax. We can, therefore, only change the parameters that we need, for example the maximum number of pages in the incoming fax (*MaxRecvPages*).

The next two parameters are important in many cases: the first allows us to use the *X3* command that configures the modem so that you don't need to wait for a dial tone to compose the number of the recipient, the second allows us to enter a default prefix to obtain, for example, a line from the PBX (eg "0")

```
ModemResultCodesCmd: ATQ0X3
ModemDialCmd: ATDP0,%s
```

The modem configuration is saved in a file named *config.ttyS0* (or *config.ttyS1* etc ... for the other ports) in the directory */etc/hylafax*. It 's a plain text file and, if necessary, we can easily change it:

```
sudo nano /etc/hylafax/config.ttyS0
```

If the modem is not detected by the setup program, we can configure it using one of the several files in */var/spool/hylafax/config*. For example, if the modem is a *Class1*, connected on *ttyS1*, the procedures to be performed are the following:

```
cd /var/spool/hylafax/config
cp class1 /etc/hylafax/config.ttyS1
cd /etc/hylafax
sudo nano config.ttyS1
```

and continue with manual configuration.

Incoming FAX

To handle incoming faxes, it is necessary that we modify a configuration file of the Hylafax service to activate *faxgetty* software. Edit the file:

```
sudo nano /etc/default/hylafax
```

and comment out the highlighted line (beware, there are two occurrences of the parameter, select the second):

```
# In a send/receive installation you must use faxgetty.
#
# To use faxmodem change the following variable value to "no".
#
# You may also run faxmodem/faxgetty via inittab instead of
# running it here from a script. In this case set its value as
# "init".
```

```
USE_FAXGETTY=yes
```

After the service restarts, even *faxgetty* starts, which takes in managing our modem waiting for incoming faxes.

Users and permissions

With Hylafax the user management and related permissions can follow his native way, or also be integrated with PAM and then LDAP. Let's look at both, because the native authentication of Hylafax may be preferable in many cases to simplify, for example, sending fax through external programs.

Native authentication

We must do it manually in three ways:

1. Add in the file */etc/hylafax/hosts.hfaxd* the IP addresses from which you can connect to Hylafax server (loopback 127.0.0.1, is set as standard, for access from the server machine itself)

2. Use the command *faxadduser*: for example, to insert the user *user1* with password *pwduser1*, run the command;

```
sudo faxadduser -p pwduser1 user1
```

3. Open to *democratic anarchy* and allow all the PCs on the network to send faxes. In */etc/hylafax/hosts.hfaxd* just add this *magic string*:

```
^.*@.*$
```

that, with wildcards, enables any user from any address. In this case, on the firewall, it is better to deny access to port 4559 used by Hylafax from the external network port!

PAM authentication

And if we want to use our usual PAM and LDAP authentication? Enjoy, we don't need to do anything since this is the default behavior of Hylafax.

Service start

Hylafax has three core services:

1. **faxq** : used to process the output queue (scheduler)
2. **hfaxd** : implements the FTP-like protocol for client server communications
3. **faxgetty** : communicates with the modem.

To restart Hylafax do as usual:

```
sudo /etc/init.d/hylafax restart
```

Please note that Ubuntu copies the modified configuration files from *etc/hylafax* to the appropriate directories automatically, for example:

```
/etc/hylafax/hosts.hfaxd → /var/spool/hylafax/etc/hosts.hfaxd
```

Management and use

Let's see some useful things to know in order to manage in the basic way this service.

Directory Structure

Hylafax creates its own directory structure where it stores its data. We see the most important folders:

/var/spool/hylafax/etc/
Contains configuration files, including the *config.ttyS0* seen before. However, with Ubuntu *we should never directly edit the files to this directory*. We must use the files in */etc/hylafax*. As we said, before the service startup files will be automatically copied to the appropriate place.

/var/spool/hylafax/sendq/
Contains faxes waiting to be sent. Is important to note a special file called *seqf* that contains the progressive number (*jobid*) of sending faxes. This number is increased by Hylafax and can be reset.

/var/spool/hylafax/recvq/
Contains received faxes in TIFF format. Even here the *seqf* file exists.

/var/spool/hylafax/doneq/
Contains reports of sent faxes

/var/spool/hylafax/docq/
Contains PS (postscript) or PDF documents of sent faxes.

/var/spool/hylafax/log/
Contains the logs for sent and received faxes.

Useful commands

Here are some useful commands for maintenance and reporting.

faxstat

The *faxstat* command gives us useful information. Without parameters it shows the state of the service, otherwise we can specify the following:

-d: shows done queue
-r: shows received queue related to incoming faxes
-s: shows send queue with pending fax jobs
-f: shows document list on PS or PDF format
-i: shows additional information about the server

faxrm

To remove a fax, we can use the *faxrm* command specifying the identification number obtained with *faxstat -s*.

faxcron

If we want a full report of sent and received faxes, we can use the command *faxcron* getting the result on the screen. We can also send the results via e-mail to sbsadmin:

```
faxcron | mail -s "HylaFAX report" sbsadmin
```

However Hylafax is already configured for this task by sending a monthly report to the *faxmaster* user. So we can simply define an alias so that sbsadmin also receive these e-mails:

```
sudo nano /etc/aliases
```

insert:

```
faxmaster:      sbsadmin
```

and refresh aliases list with:

```
newaliases
```

Maintenance

During Hylafax installation, Ubuntu already prepares the necessary for a basic system maintenance. In detail, we see that it creates two scripts, one in */etc/cron.weekly* (and so run weekly) and the other in */etc/cron.monthly* (carried out each month).

We can see what they do by editing:

```
sudo nano /etc/cron.weekly/hylafax
sudo nano /etc/cron.monthly/hylafax
```

In addition to generate a monthly report e-mailed to *faxmaster*, we can see the use of the *faxqclean* command (*weekly*) that eliminates document of the faxes sent if they are older than 35 days.

Send Fax

To send a fax we can use either the command line or a GUI clients.

Command line

To send faxes from shell we can use the *sendfax* command. If the documents are already in the *PS* or *TIFF* format, *sendfax* passes them directly to the fax server for the sending. If the file is in another format, a conversion in PS or TIFF is required. Hylafax automatically converts ASCII text files, PDF format and *SiliconGraphics* image types (*.sgi .rgb .bw .icon*). Support for all other formats can be added easily by specifying the conversion rules in */etc/hylafax/typerules*. Here are some examples:

```
sendfax -n -d <faxnumber> file
sendfax -n -d <faxnumber> -d <faxnumber2> file
sendfax -n -a "now + 30 minutes" -d <faxnumber> file
sendfax -n -D -A -t 3 -d <faxnumber> file
sendfax -n -h modem@host:4559 -d <faxnumber> file
```

where:
  -n: doen't send cover
  -d: recipient fax number
  -t: failed attempts before deleting the fax
  -D: enables e-mail notification
  -h: forces the *job* to be processed on a specific host and, optionally, using a specific modem.

Hylafax Client

If an application needs to send a fax with Hylafax, it just need to have the ability to create a Postscript file. The easiest way to do this is to use a virtual printer that allows us to save the result file to disk. The recommended print driver is the *Apple Laserwriter*, which provides a standard postscript (or its variant can also use the color if any were needed). In this way we can send all the documents produced by programs that have printing capabilities.

There are many ready-to-use clients for Hylafax, typically after creating the PS file, they allow us to enter the other information required (for example the recipient's fax number and the ability to send a cover).

A list is available at URL:

```
http://www.hylafax.org/content/Desktop_Client_Software
```

The most common is certainly *WHFC*, but I would also point out *Frogfax*, which allows to send the fax and e-mail. More informations are available at *http://www.frogfax.com*.

Incoming faxes

Incoming faxes are stored in */var/spool/hylafax/recvq*.

To view incoming faxes from any computer in local network, you can use one of the clients listed or share the directory using Samba.

After receiving the fax, Hylafax runs this custom script:

```
/var/spool/hylafax/bin/faxrcvd
```

that moves the fax in a specific directory.

Fax-to-Email Gateway

Rather than share the directory that contains the incoming faxes, we can send them in PDF format to one (or more) recipients via e-mail. To do this, simply edit the file:

```
sudo nano /var/spool/hylafax/bin/faxrcvd
```

and set:

```
SENDTO=user1,user2
FILETYPE=pdf
```

Now *user1* and *user2* will receive via e-mail as PDF attachments, all incoming faxes.

AvantFax

Developed by the official maintainers of Hylafax, *iFax Solutions Inc.*, *AvantFax* is a nice AJAX interface that provides a handy web client 2.0 to our Fax Server.

With this software developed in PHP, we can send, receive, forward and store fax, using a simple web browser. Why get up and go to the fax machine when AvantFax brings it directly into your browser window?

Installation

Unfortunately AvantFax is not present in the Ubuntu repositories, so we have to download directly from the manufacturer website and install it manually.

We go to a directory of our choice (our */home/sbsadmin* can be good), download the software (at the time of this writing is version 3.3.3) and unzip it:

```
wget http://surfnet.dl.sourceforge.net/sourceforge/avantfax/avantfax-3.3.3.tgz
tar zvxf avantfax-3.3.3.tgz
cd avantfax-3.3.3
```

Avantfax has an install script for Debian, with some minor modifications we can use to automate the installation on Ubuntu:

```
sudo nano /home/sbsadmin/avantfax-3.3.3/debian-prefs.txt
```

and modify the following values:

```
# The domain name for configuring email to fax
FAXDOMAIN=fax.stenoit.com

# if the MySQL password for root is set, specify it here
ROOTMYSQLPWD=admin
```

We've specified the domain name and root password of MySQL.

Now we modify the installation script:

```
sudo nano /home/sbsadmin/avantfax-3.3.3/debian-install.sh
```

Removing (or commenting) the following lines:

```
# CONFIGURE AVANTFAX VIRTUALHOST

#cat >> /etc/apache2/sites-enabled/000-default << EOF
#<VirtualHost *:80>
#    DocumentRoot $INSTDIR
#    ServerName avantfax
#    ErrorLog logs/avantfax-error_log
#    CustomLog logs/avantfax-access_log common
#</VirtualHost>
#EOF
```

We execute now the installation script that takes care of everything, including the installation of required packages and missing dependencies.

```
cd /home/sbsadmin/avantfax-3.3.3
sudo ./debian-install.sh
```

Using AvantFax

AvantFax is a very interesting package, we should explore it using his excellent web interface. From a machine on the network just navigate to:

```
http://sbs.stenoit.com/avantfax
```

and logon with default username and password:

```
User: admin
Password: password
```

After the first access we are required to change the admin password. After that, we can proceed with the product exploration.

15

VPN Server

A private network usually consists of dedicated and leased lines which connect multiple sites or different company locations together. The main problem of this solution is the high cost of lease and the impossibility to serve mobile users, the so-called *"road warrior"*.

So, to cut off the cost of connection, why don't use the pervasive and cheap Internet network? Unfortunately a major flaw using this network as transmission media, is the risk of data interception by unauthorized people. When the data passing through the Internet must inevitably be considered to the public domain.

A VPN (*Virtual Private Network*) solves this problem. A VPN creates an encrypted tunnel between two points that secures data traffic allowing, through the public network, to connect two entire networks or individual PCs securely as if they were connected with a dedicated and private physical wire.

Like other services seen in previous chapters, there are several products that allow us to create a VPN with Linux. Each of them has advantages and disadvantages, and they generally use very different protocols and concepts. The argument is very complex, we will try, wherever possible, to use simple concepts without getting into explanations of the OSI layer, symmetric and asymmetric keys, or other topics too technical. For this purpose there is a vast and comprehensive documentation also available online.

OpenVPN

We will use OpenVPN, a very interesting and flexible project:

✔ uses OpenSSL and can so use all their encryption algorithms

- ✔ is available for all popular software platforms (Linux, OSX, Windows etc..) both in the server and inthe client side.
- ✔ supports the shared secret key authentication, digital certificates or simple username/password also integrable with PAM.
- ✔ uses a single IP port, by default the 1194, making it easy to manage the firewall
- ✔ can use both UDP or TCP
- ✔ can work through a proxy server
- ✔ can be integrated with the NAT
- ✔ can send configuration commands to the client (eg routing, DNS server, default gateway, etc.).

We could continue, but this is already sufficient to ensure that this product is suitable for our purposes: to allow our mobile users to connect safetly from the Internet using their usual username and password and operate as if they were within the organization's network.

We will examine only two cases, both "road warriors" type with user authentication via PAM/LDAP. The first will also use digital certificates, while the second only username and password.

Installation

OpenVPN is present in the standard Ubuntu repository, so to install it we use the simple command:

```
sudo apt-get install openvpn
```

Certificates

OpenVPN comes with a set of scripts that greatly eases the creation of the certificates that we need. Copy it in the configuration directory:

```
sudo mkdir /etc/openvpn/rsa
sudo cp /usr/share/doc/openvpn/examples/easy-rsa/2.0/* /etc/openvpn/rsa/
cd /etc/openvpn/rsa
```

First we need to edit the file:

```
sudo nano /etc/openvpn/rsa/vars
```

Populating it with the default data later used by scripts to create keys and certificates. I put this at the bottom, leaving unchanged the other parameters. For example:

```
export KEY_COUNTRY="IT"
export KEY_PROVINCE="PN"
export KEY_CITY="Pordenone"
export KEY_ORG="StenoIT"
export KEY_EMAIL="sbsadmin@stenoit.com"
```

With *"sudo -s"* we become root for an indefinite amount of time, until we type *"exit"*. This is needed to run the following commands.
Prepare the environment by doing so (note dots and spaces!):

```
sudo -s
. ./vars
./clean-all
```

The first command (*. . /vars),* must be executed every time we open a shell bash to create certificates. The second (*./clean-all*), which removes all the old keys and create the directory */etc/openvpn/rsa/keys*, only the first time.

Certification Authority

Preparing the certificate of our own *Certification Authority* using:

```
./build-ca
```

We can leave all the defaults proposed. This script will output the files:

```
/etc/openvpn/keys/ca.crt
/etc/openvpn/keys/ca.key
```

That are the certificate and the key of the Certification Authority (CA).

Server certificates and keys

Go forward with the creation of the keys to our server:

```
./build-key-server sbs
```

Where *"sbs"* is the name of our server that will be proposed by the script as *"Common Name"* which, as we have seen in the previous chapters, must be unique. Also here we leave the defaults and answer *"y"* to requests for *"sign"* the certificate. These files are created:

```
/etc/openvpn/keys/sbs.crt
/etc/openvpn/keys/sbs.key
```

Diffie Hellman

Now we generate the *"Diffie Hellman"* parameters which, in short, allow us to negotiate a secure connection through an insecure channel. This process takes a bit of time.

```
./build-dh
```

at the end we will have the file:

```
/etc/openvpn/keys/dh1024.pem
```

SSL/TLS key

This step is not required but useful. It allows us to be sure of the identity of the server we're connecting. Generate the key:

```
openvpn --genkey --secret ta.key
```

obtaining the file:

```
/etc/openvpn/rsa/ta.key
```

Clients certificates and keys

Now we are ready to create certificates and keys of the clients that connect to our server. We create them without a password since it will use PAM authentication.

```
./build-key client1
```

Where *"client1"* is the unique name of a computer/user that will access to our network through the VPN. As for the server certificate, *"client1"* will be proposed as unique *"Common Name"*. Also here we leave the values proposed by the script and answer *"y"* when prompted to *"sign"*.

The files created are as follows:

```
/etc/openvpn/keys/client1.crt
/etc/openvpn/keys/client1.key
```

Now, in the same way, we can proceed in the generation of other certificates by simply repeating the procedure::

```
./build-key client2
./build-key client3
```

and so on. Always remember that the names must be unique. A good technique if they are members of our domain, is to use the netbios and DNS name of the PC.

Now we can exit from root mode with a simple:

```
exit
```

Target of certificates and keys

It is always difficult to remember what to do now with the generated files. What we see now is a useful table that shows what are these files and those who need them.

Files that are labeled as "secret" should not be sent to users over insecure channels (like a common mail) but delivered through reliable methods.

File	Needed by	Purpose	Secret
ca.crt	Server and Clients	Certificate for root CA	NO
ca.key	Server only	Key for root CA	YES
dh1024.pem	Server only	Diffie Hellman parameters	NO
sbs.crt	Server only	Server Certificate	NO
sbs.key	Server only	Server Key	YES
ta.key	Server and Clients	Server SSL/TLS Auth key	YES
client1.crt	Client1 only	Client1 certificate	NO
client1.key	Client1 only	Client1 key	YES

Let's start from the server, copying the files in their right place:

```
sudo cp /etc/openvpn/rsa/keys/dh1024.pem /etc/openvpn/
sudo cp /etc/openvpn/rsa/keys/ca.crt /etc/openvpn/
sudo cp /etc/openvpn/rsa/keys/ca.key /etc/openvpn/
sudo cp /etc/openvpn/rsa/keys/sbs.key /etc/openvpn/
sudo cp /etc/openvpn/rsa/keys/sbs.crt /etc/openvpn/
sudo cp /etc/openvpn/rsa/ta.key /etc/openvpn/
```

Following the table we can already identify what are the files that I'll have to give also to the *client1* and which of them, shown here, are to be kept *"secrets"*:

```
ca.crt
ta.key
client1.crt
client1.key
```

Fundamentals

Without going too deep, we now analyze three fundamental concepts that show us how OpenVPN works, and required to decide how to configure our VPN.

UDP or TCP?

OpenVPN can establish communications using both Internet protocols. There is no absolute best solution, there is only the best solution for the type of communication that I have to establish through the VPN tunnel. To understand, we see their differences.

UDP is a connectionless protocol. When you a send a data or message, you don't know if it'll get there, it could get lost on the way. There may be corruption while transferring a message.

TCP is a connection-oriented protocol. When a file or message send it, it will be delivered unless connections fails. If the connection is lost, the server will request the lost part. There is no corruption while transferring a message.

The use of TCP compared to UDP is generally preferred when you need to have guarantees on data delivery or the order of arrival of several segments, such as in the case of file transfers. Instead UDP is mainly used when the interaction between the two hosts must be fast and the guarantee of transmission is not essential. The loss of a few frames, for example, does not affect the transmission of a video or audio stream.

In our case we will use TCP.

TUN or TAP?

OpenVPN, to work its communications, creates a **virtual network interface** that can be of two types: *TUN* or *TAP*. Let us see the differences.

TUN device creates a *point-to-point* communication, for a comparison think about a sort of modem connection, and routes *IP protocol frames*.

TAP, instead, creates a *true virtual network adapter* on which *Ethernet frames and then virtually any protocol* are routed.

In our case we will use TAP.

Bridge or Router?

OpenVPN can be configured to create a *bridge* between the local and remote network, or to leave them separate and work in *routing*.

Creating a bridge, *the two networks are merged* and they will use the same address space. In our example, the *eth0* device would be "fused" with *tap0* (is not possible to use the bridge with TUN devices) into a new entity called *br0*, which became my virtual network adapter.

In bridge, then, the remote client, when connected, is part of our network at ethernet level, and will have an address 192.168.20.x as our PC network. The main consequence of this is that the broadcast can reach all the machines (local and remote), and so many network protocols which base their working on it (such as Samba SMB) operate in a transparent manner with the bridged mode.

A client in routing, instead, is part of a different network. In our example, remote clients will have an address in the form 192.168.30.x and will be separated from local clients from the router (in our case corresponds to the firewall and the server).

We may therefore think that it is preferable the bridged mode, but it is not always true. The bridge does not scale, does not allow a granular privilege management, and the OpenVPN configuration is more complicated. I prefer routed networks because I believe they are more organized and manageable. Here we use routed mode.

Configuration with user/password and certificates

After we created the required SSL certificates and understood the basic concepts, we can proceed with the configuration of the OpenVPN server and client using only the bare minimum for our purposes. Otherwise, for special configurations, we can refer to the help that we find on the official website of the project.

We begin with the more secure configuration, that provides user and password combined with the personal certificate for each client.

Server

We create the configuration file for the server side:

```
sudo nano /etc/openvpn/server.conf
```

with this:

```
port 1194
proto tcp
dev tap

ca /etc/openvpn/ca.crt
cert /etc/openvpn/sbs.crt
key /etc/openvpn/sbs.key
dh /etc/openvpn/dh1024.pem
tls-auth /etc/openvpn/ta.key 0
cipher AES-128-CBC

server 192.168.30.0 255.255.255.0
ifconfig-pool-persist ipp.txt
push "route 192.168.20.0 255.255.255.0"
push "dhcp-option DNS 192.168.20.1"
push "dhcp-option WINS 192.168.20.1"
client-to-client
keepalive 10 120
comp-lzo
max-clients 5
user nobody
persist-key
persist-tun
log-append /var/log/openvpn.log
verb 3

# authentication plugin
plugin /usr/lib/openvpn/openvpn-auth-pam.so login
```

The purpose of most of the parameters is easy to understand, as the port (1194), the protocol to use (TCP), the type of device (tap) and the part relating to certificates and data encryption.

The *server* parameter defines the subnet of remote clients that in our case will be 192.168.30.x.

With *ifconfig-pool-persist*, OpenVPN stores in a file (*ipp.txt*) the allocated IP. In this way a remote client will have, if possible, always the same address.

The *push* commands are used to assign values to the configuration of the client's network. For example given them the *route* to the internal network and DNS and WINS IP that are important for Samba work.

The parameter *client-to-client* makes sure that the remote clients can reach each other, *comp-lzo* compresses the data in transit and *max-clients* defines the maximum number of concurrent connections.

The last line is important for us: it activates the PAM authentication plugin configured with */etc/pam.d/login*. In this way, remote users will use the same username and password they use for other services. In short, still *Single-Signon*.

Now we just have to restart the service:

```
sudo /etc/init.d/openvpn restart
```

Our server is ready and we can control the network interfaces available now:

```
ifconfig
```

In addition to *eth0* and *eth1*, we should now see the new virtual interface *tap0* created by OpenVPN:

```
tap0      Link encap:Ethernet  HWaddr 00:ff:22:8e:de:c6
          inet addr:192.168.30.1  Bcast:192.168.30.255  Mask:255.255.255.0
          inet6 addr: fe80::2ff:22ff:fe8e:dec6/64 Scope:Link
          UP BROADCAST RUNNING MULTICAST  MTU:1500  Metric:1
          RX packets:2283 errors:0 dropped:0 overruns:0 frame:0
          TX packets:1332 errors:0 dropped:0 overruns:0 carrier:0
          collisions:0 txqueuelen:100
          RX bytes:181178 (176.9 KB)  TX bytes:121737 (118.8 KB)
```

ready to use.

Firewall

We need to configure our firewall to manage our VPN. Basically we have a new interface and a new zone to manage. For details, refer to Chapter 6.

Then add the newcomer:

```
sudo nano /etc/shorewall/interfaces
```

in this manner:

```
#ZONE INTERFACE BCAST   OPTIONS
net   eth0      detect  tcpflags,routefilter,nosmurfs,logmartians
loc   eth1      detect  dhcp,tcpflags,nosmurfs,routeback
vpn   tap0      -       dhcp,tcpflags,nosmurfs,routeback
#LAST LINE -- ADD YOUR ENTRIES BEFORE THIS ONE -- DO NOT REMOVE
```

continue with "zone" files:

```
sudo nano /etc/shorewall/zones
```

adding to the end the zone *"vpn"*:

```
fw      firewall
net     ipv4
loc     ipv4
vpn     ipv4
```

We create the file for *"tunnels"*:

```
sudo nano /etc/shorewall/tunnels
```

inserting:

```
#TYPE                  ZONE    GATEWAY         GATEWAY
#                                              ZONE
openvpnserver          net     0.0.0.0/0
#LAST LINE -- ADD YOUR ENTRIES BEFORE THIS ONE -- DO NOT REMOVE
```

Now we must edit the default policy file of the firewall, because it includes the traffic to and from our new zone *"vpn"*:

```
sudo nano /etc/shorewall/policy
```

insert (be careful to order) the following highlighted rules:

```
loc     net     ACCEPT
loc     $FW     ACCEPT
loc     vpn     ACCEPT
loc     all     REJECT          info

vpn     net     ACCEPT
vpn     $FW     ACCEPT
vpn     loc     ACCEPT
vpn     all     REJECT          info

$FW     net     ACCEPT
$FW     loc     ACCEPT
$FW     vpn     ACCEPT
$FW     all     REJECT          info

net     $FW     DROP            info
net     loc     DROP            info
net     vpn     DROP            info
net     all     DROP            info

all     all     REJECT          info
```

and restart the firewall:

```
sudo shorewall restart
```

Now our server is ready for connections.

Client

The configuration file of OpenVPN client is virtually the same by using Windows rather than Linux or OSX. The difference is, of course, the GUI, but when used from the command line, the syntax is the same. In our case we will see how to configure a Windows client.

Installation

We must download the latest client (at the time of this writing is 2.1.4) that works also with Windows Vista and Seven, from here:

```
http://www.openvpn.net/index.php/downloads.html
```

The setup creates the virtual network interface TUN/TAP and install the *OpenVPN-GUI* front end. Copy the SSL certificates and keys for *client1* in this folder:

```
c:\program files\openvpn\config
```

remember that files are:

```
ca.crt
ta.key
client1.crt
client1.key
```

With a text editor (the default Notepad is OK) write the client configuration:

```
client
dev tap
proto tcp
remote 212.239.29.208 1194
resolv-retry infinite
nobind
persist-key
persist-tun

ca ca.crt
cert user1.crt
key user1.key
ns-cert-type server
tls-client
tls-auth ta.key 1
cipher AES-128-CBC

comp-lzo
verb 3

auth-user-pass
```

Save as *sbs.ovpn* here:

```
c:\program files\openvpn\config\sbs.ovpn
```

Here, as in the case of the server, the purpose of parameters is easily understood. *client* indicates that this is a configuration of this type, *remote* indicates the server address and port to use for the connection. Then there are the parameters of the certificates and encryption keys used. Important to the bottom line, *auth-user-pass*, which means that I want to use authentication with username and password.

The desktop should have the icon to run the OpenVPN GUI. If you have Windows Vista and UAC enabled (it should never be disabled unless absolutely necessary) before you run it, however, we must set it to run with administrative privileges. Just right-click the icon, select *Properties> Compatibility* and check the *"Run this program as administrator"*.

OpenVPN GUI goes in the Windows tray area: clicking on it with the right mouse button you should see a small menu with *"Connect"*.

Starting the connection using your username and password, after a while we should be connected with an IP 192.168.30.x. Well, the tunnel has been established.

Configuration with user/password only

We can simplify the configuration slightly sacrificing security. In this way is sufficient to have only server certificates. For each client, then, we will copy the same files: Certification Authority (*ca.crt*) and, if used, the TLS (*ta.key*).

The firewall configuration and the installation and operation of the client remains unchanged.

Server

This is the new configuration file, with the differences highlighted in the bottom:

```
port 1194
proto tcp
dev tap

ca /etc/openvpn/ca.crt
cert /etc/openvpn/sbs.crt
key /etc/openvpn/sbs.key
dh /etc/openvpn/dh1024.pem
tls-auth /etc/openvpn/ta.key 0
cipher AES-128-CBC

server 192.168.30.0 255.255.255.0
ifconfig-pool-persist ipp.txt
push "route 192.168.20.0 255.255.255.0"
push "dhcp-option DNS 192.168.20.1"
push "dhcp-option WINS 192.168.20.1"
client-to-client
keepalive 10 120
comp-lzo
```

```
max-clients 5
user nobody
persist-key
persist-tun
log-append /var/log/openvpn.log
verb 3

# authentication plugin
plugin /usr/lib/openvpn/openvpn-auth-pam.so login
client-cert-not-required
username-as-common-name
```

The parameter *client-cert-not-required* indicates that for the VPN connection the client personal certificate is not necessary, and *username-as-common-name* that the user name is used as *"Common Name"*.

The *"Common Name"* is also used in the log and in the *ipp.txt* file to store user-IP address associations.

Client

The client configuration is easier because we no longer need to create their personal certificates. The required files are, so, only two and the same for everyone:

```
ca.crt
ta.key
```

The configuration file is virtually the same as before, but without, of course, the client certificates part:

```
client
dev tap
proto tcp
remote 212.239.29.208 1194
resolv-retry infinite
nobind
persist-key
persist-tun

ca ca.crt
ns-cert-type server
tls-client
tls-auth ta.key 1
cipher AES-128-CBC

comp-lzo
verb 3

auth-user-pass
```

Insight

A VPN is a very interesting solution, and OpenVPN in this case a real Swiss boxcutter.

In this chapter we have considered only a small par of the possibilities that are offered. For example we do not have at least consider the argument *LAN-to-LAN* that allows us to interconnect networks that are geographically dispersed, not only an individual user (*road warriors*).

The topic is huge and complex, but for our purposes what has been done by now is enough.

16
Conclusions

We have done a great job. On this trip we learned how to create, with Ubuntu Server 10.04, a true *Small Business Server* that brilliantly solves many of the typical requests that can reach us today by a small, or less small, business.

We must remember, above all, that we have created everything using only *Open Source* software, freely available to all. For this reason we must especially thanks the volunteers, businesses, academic institutions and others, that, with their great passion and skill have made this software complete, efficient and free, spreading, at the same time, the knowledge to the four corners of the planet.

Many thanks to all.

Probably will not happen often to centralize all of its services on a single machine, but the versatility and scalability of LDAP will allow us to easily divide tasks among multiple servers with minimal changes at the seen configuration, making the network infrastructure more secure and balanced.

Links

We add, finally, a list of links where we could get extensive documentation on what we saw. Once again, Internet, is the true great source of knowledge available to us.

Ubuntu	http://www.ubuntu.com
	https://help.ubuntu.com/10.04/serverguide/C/index.html
	http://www.canonical.com
Debian	http://www.debian.org
Wikipedia	http://www.wikipedia.org/
OpenSSH	http://www.openssh.com/
OpenLDAP	http://www.openldap.org/

Dnsmasq	http://www.thekelleys.org.uk/dnsmasq/doc.html
Shorewall	http://www.shorewall.net/
Apache	http://www.apache.org/
MySQL	http://www.mysql.com/
PHP	http://www.php.net/
Samba	http://www.samba.org
smbldap-tools	http://www.iallanis.info/
ACL Posix	http://www.suse.de/~agruen/acl/linux-acls/online/
LDAP Manager	http://lam.sourceforge.net/
LDAP Admin	http://ldapadmin.sourceforge.net/
MS UsrMgr.exe	http://www.microsoft.com/
Postfix	http://www.postfix.org/
Postgrey	http://postgrey.schweikert.ch/
Amavis	http://www.amavis.org/
	http://www.ijs.si/software/amavisd/
Spamassassin	http://spamassassin.apache.org/
ClamAV	http://www.clamav.net/
Dovecot	http://www.dovecot.org/
Roundcube	http://www.roundcube.net/
Squid	http://www.squid-cache.org/
WPAD	http://en.wikipedia.org/wiki/Wpad
OpenNTPD	http://www.openntpd.org/
Rsnapshot	http://www.rsnapshot.org/
Jabber	http://www.jabber.org
	http://codex.xiaoka.com/wiki/jabberd2:start
	http://www.jabberdoc.com/
MUC	https://gna.org/projects/mu-conference
Openfire	http://www.igniterealtime.org/
PSI	http://psi-im.org/
Hylafax	http://www.hylafax.org/
Frogfax	http://www.frogfax.com/
WHFC	http://whfc.uli-eckhardt.de/
AvantFAX	http://www.avantfax.com/
OpenVPN	http://openvpn.net/